SPEAK ON PURPOSE

Deliver Your Message

Precisely & Effectively

A Primer on Sales Communication

Praise for the SPEAK ON PURPOSE Primer & Training Curriculum

...on the Primer

"Marlōn Hall is an authority in today's culture on speaking and how to do it well. He does a great job encapsulating and capturing his message and writing it powerfully and succinctly. A great read and a must have."

-Phillip W. Koontz, Former US Navy Seal, Author of "The Truth Behind My Trident"

...on the Training Curriculum

"Thank you so much for your inspiration! I presented The Apple Pie to our team and we have successfully used it to reach our goals! You made me look like a Super Star! Thank you!"

-M. Evans, Credit Union Member Consultant

SPEAK ON PURPOSE: Deliver Your Message Precisely & Effectively

A Primer on Sales Communication

by Marlōn Hall, AS, BS, CFS

Foreword by Mark Zinder

Kindle Direct Publishing

USA

Speak On Purpose:

Deliver Your Message Precisely & Effectively

A Primer on Sales Communication

by Marlōn Hall, AS, BS, CFS

Copyright © 2019 by Marlōn Hall

ISBN: 9781093284003

Printed in the United States of America

Published via Kindle Direct Publishing

Direct orders/inquiries to: speakonpurpose@gmail.com

This book is dedicated to

Ares, insatiable in battle. The god of war who resides on Olympus

&

Rameses, born of Ra, creator of all things, god of the sun.

The avatar who resides on Earth.

This page intentionally left blank.

Table of Contents

FOREWORD

by Mark Zinder

When I was a child, I had a speech impediment. Later in life I was told, "It's not what you say, but how you say it." That's not entirely true if you have a lisp, I must add!

I grew up in an era when childhood bullying, brought on by the slightest defect, was more the rule rather than the exception. For my protection, and to help me overcome my lisp, my parents saw fit to enroll me in acting and speech lessons. The jury is still out on whether it was to save *me* from embarrassment or *them*.

I was taught how to overcome my impediment and along the way I learned numerous techniques and skills for proper 'speech communication.' I learned voice inflection, non-verbal pauses (pausing without filling the empty space with an "uh" or a "you know"), oral interpretation, voice projection, elocution and stage movement…to name a few. Today, after I finish speaking to a large group, sometimes an individual will approach me with great curiosity, asking, "How do you do it?" They can't quite put their finger on it, but they know they've witnessed a performance unlike any other presentation they've heard in their lifetime. How did I say, what I was contracted to say, connect with the audience and maintain a level of interest that kept everyone on the edge of their seats wanting more? That's the question…how do you do that?

It's all in the technique, and like so many other things in life, there are techniques that we can employ to help us improve. The problem is, rarely are we taught communication *skills*. Few of us go to school to major in something called 'speech communication,' my very focus. Why in the world would anyone spend their valuable financial resources to learn how to do something that they already know how to do? Maybe because we were never actually taught to do it correctly, we just picked it up along the way.

In this book, written by Marlōn Hall, a friend and colleague of mine, you will find many techniques that, when learned, practiced and incorporated, will take your communication skills to the next level. As with nearly everything else in this world, only when you discover that the tools exist will you be able to put them to use and achieve a greater degree of success in whatever you are trying to learn and perfect. In this book, you will discover many tools. In fact, you will learn that how you say it is just as important as what you say! Speak on purpose!

Mark Zinder is a keynote speaker who has delivered thousands of presentations around the world, to hundreds of thousands of individuals. Visit http://www.markzinder.com for more information.

INTRODUCTION

Much of the following is written in the voice of a professional trainer speaking to a class of financial institution employees—tellers and lenders, board members and CEOs—all of whom are in training. This is because I developed, collected and researched much of the book's content while training diverse audiences of bank and credit union employees, in many places over many years. As a result, individuals working in financial institutions, the financial services industry at-large and sales and marketing departments in any industry, may be able to comprehend and apply many of the concepts laid out in this book immediately. At the same time, the concepts outlined herein apply equally well to anyone interacting with customers in any capacity and in any setting where you would simply like to communicate more effectively, be it with friends, family, teachers, students, employees, managers, colleagues, constituents, etc.

Why read this book? You already speak on purpose, right? No, you do not. According to Charles Duhigg, author of "The Power of Habit" (2014), our brains automate between 40% to 95% of our actions to save energy. You are on autopilot. If you are not experiencing ideal outcomes as a result of every one of your conversations, discussions and presentations, your auto pilot's communication coding may be faulty. Move closer to where you want to be by programming the words you write and type, the words coming out of your mouth and your mannerisms. You can control how you communicate. Control what you can control.

MODULE 1: Hierarchy of Communication

As up-and-coming sales professionals, we are repeatedly told by our trainers, mentors and managers that a call is better than an email, a virtual meeting is better than a call and an in-person meeting is better than all of these.

Ok, but why?

Some of us instantly 'get it' or take this at face value. Even so, we all remain susceptible to not following this advice at any given moment. In an effort to minimize backsliding toward less effective means of communication, here we will examine why this oft-shared wisdom bears out.

1.1   Something Is Better Than Nothing

In the hierarchy of communication, some forms of communication are more effective than others. To start, we must establish a baseline. The baseline in communication (and in sales) is at the bottom of the hierarchy or the bottom step of a ladder (*see figure 1*). This bottom step is our least effective method of communication. NO COMMUNICATION. While this may seem obvious, consider what happens when you simply do not pick up the phone and do not make the call. It happens all the time. There is some excuse or distraction and then, before you know it, it is day's end and you will do it tomorrow…or it is week's end and you will do it next week. Maybe. Regardless, you were the least effective at delivering your message today…because you did not deliver it.

If for some reason you do not want to deliver a message, so be it. Speak on purpose and make that inaction your decision, not an accident.

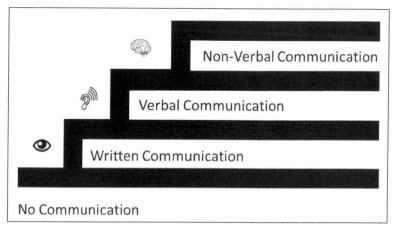

Figure 1

1.2   Is What You See What You Get?

The next step up the ladder is WRITTEN COMMUNICATION. To be clear, while written communication rests near the bottom of the hierarchy of effective communication, relatively speaking it is orders of magnitude better than no communication at all. If you have not heard from someone in a while, do you enjoy receiving a postcard from them? Of course you do! That said, written communication often does not register at all. As consumers we are inundated with disclosures, forms, fine print, emails, signage and many other written messages. Frequently these messages are poorly designed, especially in the realms of finance and sales.

Wherever you are standing or sitting right now, look around for a sign. Do you see one, large or small? A business' sign? A street sign? Right now, as I am writing this in my basement, I see the spine of a book, the cover of a magazine, a label on a piece of packaging and a poster on a wall. All of these are things in my peripheral vision of course, my laptop is directly in front of me. I was not consciously aware of these 'signs' until I sought them out just now.

Were you conscious of the messages that were being conveyed by the writings you see around you? Doubtful. Until you specifically sought them out, these messages were all—for the most part—ineffective. Better than nothing, of course, because if you had sought them out and they were not there, you would have found nothing.

Much research has been done by academic psychologists on the effect of signage on human behavior. The factors involved in sign effectiveness are myriad (context, content, design, sender-receiver relationship, receiver mindset, etc.) Some factors we can control, many we cannot. Branch employees rarely determine the content, volume and placement of signs in their branch.

1.3   What's Your Sign?

When conducting Speak On Purpose training in financial centers, I often look for and find signage strategically placed on the wall behind a banker's desk or the teller line. The signage is often large and colorful and sometimes dynamic (i.e. – video screens or LED marquees). The signage generally hangs in clear view of a customer sitting in front of the desk facing the banker or standing at the teller line facing the teller. Presumably, the corporate marketing department placed and designed the written signage to be what Meis and Kashima,[1] from the Melbourne School of Psychological Sciences, call "stationary, persuasive communication" (2017).

If your desk has a sign on the wall behind you, the next time you are finished helping a customer, as a courtesy, walk them all the way to the branch exit—preferably out of view of your office. Then ask them to tell you any one word that was written on the sign behind your desk. If you like, ask them to, without looking around, tell you any one word on any sign in the financial center. If they cannot, if they do not recall seeing a sign, if they provide an incorrect answer, or if it takes them a long time and much effort to recall anything, you will see why written communication rests near the bottom of the hierarchy of effective communication. Generally, unless they are actively looking for something, people do not read signs.

Need more proof? Ask a veteran bank employee if anyone has ever walked into the bank and asked them, "What bank is this?" or "Is this a bank?"

Again, written communication still has its uses! Clearly, written communication is often required for compliance, used to standardize messaging and used to foster convenience, portability and permanence. It is easy to mail, leave behind as a reminder, and use as a speaker's prop. These are all examples of using written communication to speak on purpose. Exercise as much control over your written messaging as you can, while remembering that, as we move up the hierarchy of effective communication, written communication remains firmly near the bottom.

In 1885, Thomas Smith wrote in his treatise on marketing, "Successful Advertising"[2], that it takes a prospect at least 20 exposures to a written ad before he or she will purchase the item being advertised (*see figure 2*).

The 1st time people look at an ad, they don't see it.
The 2nd time, they don't notice it.
The 3rd time, they are aware that it is there.
The 4th time, they have a fleeting sense that they've seen it before.
The 5th time, they actually read the ad.
The 6th time, they thumb their nose at it.
The 7th time, they get a little irritated with it.
The 8th time, they think, "Here's that confounded ad again."
The 9th time, they wonder if they're missing out on something.
The 10th time, they ask their friends or neighbors if they've tried it.
The 11th time, they wonder how the company is paying for all these ads.
The 12th time, they start to think that it must be a good product.
The 13th time, they start to feel the product has value.
The 14th time, they start to feel like they've wanted a product like this for a long time.
The 15th time, they start to yearn for it because they can't afford to buy it.
The 16th time, they accept the fact that they will buy it sometime in the future.
The 17th time, they make a commitment to buy the product.
The 18th time, they curse their poverty because they can't buy this terrific product.
The 19th time, they count their money very carefully.
The 20th time prospects see the ad, they buy what it is offering.

-Smith, 1885

Figure 2

Smith's guidance from over a century ago remains relevant today. Marketers call this progression *effective frequency*; the number of exposures required to get the desired result. Microsoft conducted a study[3] that confirmed Smith's 20 exposure rule for print advertising and subsequent research by cognitive scientists and educators found that adding audio to your messaging brings its effective frequency down to 14 exposures.

1.4   Say Something!

Speaking of audio, the next step up the ladder of effective communication is VERBAL COMMUNICATION. One of the simplest ways to demonstrate the effectiveness of verbal communication relative to written communication is outlined in the situation that follows. This scenario is so common, nearly any business person will attest to having experienced it.

Something is written down or typed on a piece of paper. It has been delivered to the customer with whom you are speaking. While speaking, you deliver a message somewhat, or even completely, at odds with what is written down. The reason you deliver a contrary message does not matter. The customer with whom you are speaking may sign the paper, look at it and take it with him or her. When you follow up with the customer an hour from now (or a day from now, a week now or even a month from now) what is he or she more likely to recall? What was said; not what was written. If the customer seeks to hold you accountable for what was communicated, on which communication method is he or she most likely to focus? Verbal communication, what was said! (Lawyers notwithstanding.)

This phenomenon is not your imagination. Our long-term memory processes verbal information differently from written information. Verbal messages are encoded and strengthened in our memories after we sleep (Frost & Monaghan, 2017). Not only are verbal messages easier to recall due to cognitive mechanics, people simply like it when you talk to them and generally prefer verbal communication to written communication (Fawcett & Oldfield, 2016). A 2016 study of the effectiveness of verbal feedback versus written feedback for professors providing feedback to college students found that students felt an impulse to respond to verbal feedback. They also reported a strengthened relationship with the professor. As a matter of fact, 98.3% of respondents reported that verbal feedback made them feel more appreciated than written feedback (Knauf, 2016).

Consider your customer relationships and sales objectives. Now consider the differences between no communication, written communication and verbal communication we have already covered. Likely, you want to strengthen your relationships and achieve your objectives. Speaking on purpose at each level of the hierarchy of communication helps you reduce effective frequency and leaves clients feeling more appreciated. Indeed, feelings are at the crux of the final step up the communication ladder. The final step up the ladder is NONVERBAL COMMUNICATION.

1.5 Read & Write Between the Lines

Imagine you are talking to a teenage boy, like my son. Behind him there hangs a clearly legible poster in all caps reading: "I AM LISTENING TO YOU." In addition, the young man says to you as you settle in to give him a lecture, "I am listening to you." Having provided both a legible (purposeful even!) written message you cannot miss and a verbal message you understood clearly, the teen proceeds to chew gum, look down at his phone and turn slightly away from you as you begin to speak. Is this teenager truly listening to you?

His nonverbal communications say NO! And as a human being, non-verbal communication outweighs all other types of messages combined. Body language, macro & micro-expressions (250 milliseconds or less[4]), tone, eye contact, hand movements…there are innumerable ways to enhance or destroy the efficacy of your other communication methods. In reality, you can often convey far more nonverbally than you could with any number of signs or words (Martinez, Falvello, Aviezer & Todorov, 2016).

You may have read the book (or seen a t-shirt inspired by) Robert Fulghum's 2004 bestseller; "All I Really Need to Know I Learned in Kindergarten." Around that age your teacher or parent or scout leader may have told you (all three told me), "Look at me when I talk to you!" and/or, "Face me when you speak to me!" and/or, "Stand and sit up straight!" You (like me) may have even been told why—that doing so denotes respect. It is true, the body language your guardians insisted upon does denote respect, amongst other things. When you speak on purpose with your posture and body language while someone is speaking to you, you can convey your respect for that person far more effectively than a sign or a statement expressing your respect.

Whereas countless anecdotes shared by my clients and my own years of experience in sales and public speaking have confirmed this, Princeton researchers and many others have also found that, "…body language may convey compelling emotional cues which influence, and at times, even overwrite facial emotion recognition." (Martinez, et. al. 2016).

Let's examine some effective means of nonverbal communication you may not be utilizing on purpose. When you make direct eye contact with someone who is speaking, you convey to them, amongst other things, that you are hearing him or her. Your eyes are directed at them, as are your ears which do the hearing. When you direct your entire body (not only your eyes and ears) toward the speaker, you generally convey that you are fully engaged, you are hearing and listening. When you nod your head at the speaker, you can convey comprehension of their message.

The speaker's direct and peripheral vision—direct conduits to their subconscious—pick up on all of these signals. Anyone in a marriage or relationship can tell you there is a clear distinction between hearing, listening and comprehension. Whether you are seeking to impact a professional relationship or a personal relationship, speak on purpose and utilize these tactics with each goal in mind.

Want more? Sharon Hand, my favorite communications instructor in college, advised opening your posture by keeping your arms uncrossed, keeping your hands out of your pockets and keeping your toes pointing slightly outward when you are the speaker. Draw your audience in, versus blocking them out, with your body language

(LCCC, 2001). Lean slightly forward when you are listening, to convey that you are particularly interested in the speaker and/or their topic. Speaking on purpose with nonverbal communication is the physical equivalent of reading and writing between the lines. There are entire books available, far lengthier than this one, dedicated solely to nonverbal communication, including body language, micro expressions and more. Pick one up! Books such as these will definitely help you speak on purpose.

1.6   Stop Yelling

Though you may have first become aware of some of these nonverbal tools in kindergarten like I did, I picked up this particularly ingenious application of nonverbal messaging in college while working at a call center. We handled inbound calls for Time Warner Cable® of New York City, Canon® Copiers, America Online® (AOL®) and Starz® Movie Channel. The cable customers were often among the angriest when we initially answered the phone. If the customer had taken a day off from work and waited hours for a cable repair technician to arrive and the technician never arrived, the customer could go from zero-to-100 on the anger meter in no time. Trying to get a word in edgewise with those customers, under those circumstances, was often a challenge. I sometimes saw and heard call center agents get visibly upset themselves, transferring customers to supervisors or even (rarely and sadly) hanging up on customers once the agent determined the customer would not stop yelling.

A wily call center veteran gave me a tip that I recall, and use in other situations, to this day. When people called in yelling, immediately upon answering the call, he would patiently wait for the inevitable pause as the caller took a breath. At that pause he would calmly insert, "Alright Mr. Johnson, let me write that down." He would then pick up a pen and clipboard, hold them near his headset microphone and make writing sounds into the microphone. Instantly, the caller would stop their tirade. My veteran co-worker told me this technique worked for him 100% of the time. The purpose of his technique was simple, create a point in the call where he could begin moving toward a solution. While making writing sounds on a clipboard did not solve anything, neither did the customer's endless yelling.

I plugged in with him at his cubicle several times and watched him use this maneuver repeatedly. It really did work for him every time. I tested it myself, alternating between using the maneuver with angry callers and not doing so. I changed my verbiage to, "Let me type that in," and made loud keyboard clicks as I typed (this was not effective). Ultimately I found that only when I used the technique as taught, was I able to move toward a solution straightaway. When I did not use it, people sometimes yelled themselves hoarse. (Note: People will yell non-stop for a very long time if you let them.)

A cursory analysis of this particular Speak On Purpose technique suggests that the angry customer pauses when you state, "Let me write this down," because common sense dictates pausing their rant allows you to better concentrate and record what they have communicated thus far, a win for them. Once the momentum of their tirade is broken, it is easier for you to prevent it from starting again by effectively communicating your efforts to solve the problem. Solving the problem is their primary purpose in contacting you. Finally, speaking on purpose with a calm yet determined demeanor can nicely offset the customers agitated demeanor and again, help move them toward solving the problem instead of yelling about it.

Later in life, I found this maneuver was applicable in face-to-face meetings as well. Anytime I pulled out a pen and pad of paper and started jotting down what people were saying, their reactions visibly improved.

1.7 Non-Bank Stress Tests

In banking, there are stress tests. A true stress test of the writing-it-down technique can be held the next time you are in a particularly nasty argument with your significant other. When he or she pauses to catch a breath after incessantly yelling and you are ready to start yelling—because you were simply waiting for your turn to talk (or yell?)—whip out a notepad and a pen instead. Stop the argument's momentum by saying, "Alright honey, let me write that down."

To avoid having something thrown at your head, be absolutely sincere and not even remotely sarcastic.

When used in this context, the technique may result in some humor. Regardless, it will generally have the effect of hitting a pause button on the argument. If you sincerely want to solve the problem you are arguing about, hitting pause may be of great value. People yelling at each other are often not hearing, listening to, or understanding each other. The nonverbal maneuver of writing-it-down works by communicating, "Not only am I hearing you and listening to you, what you are saying is IMPORTANT to me." This is why writing-it-down has such an impact on the phone, across a desk, or in an argument. In all of these circumstances, obviously speakers want to be heard and listened to. What may be less obvious is how you would make a speaker feel if you conveyed that, upon hearing & listening, you find his or her words to be important enough for you to record them. That is a wonderful feeling for the speaker that registers immediately in their subconscious. You can manufacture this wonderful feeling when you speak on purpose.

1.8   Take It to the Bank

Imagine a customer with multiple banking relationships interacting with each bank for different needs. Every time the customer interacts with your bank, however, each employee is trained (whether on the phone, at the teller line, at the drive through or across the desk) to always write down what the customer says. That customer may not be able to articulate why, but when surveyed he or she expresses really good feelings about interacting with your bank.

Under these circumstances, when you introduce a new concept or colleague, is the customer more likely to react positively to that effort? Yes. When the time comes to consolidate assets to one bank later in life—as so many older Americans do—is the customer more likely to consolidate with the bank that consistently made him or her feel the best? Yes. Will the customer, if asked, refer his or her friends and family to the bank that effectively communicated how important the customer was to it? Yes!

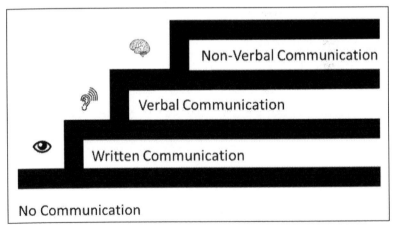

Figure 1

Whichever level of the hierarchy (*see figure 1*), or combination of levels, you use to speak to your customers in any given circumstance, speak on purpose!

1.9   Reflections on Module 1

When you, your team or your organization speak on purpose you may develop a competitive advantage based on the fact that your competitors do not.

* It has been widely reported (*see the various articles below*) that later in life, near retirement age, customers often consolidate most of their banking and financial services relationships into a single relationship with one institution. Part of this consolidation may result from retirees' plans to travel more during retirement. Managing a multitude of financial services relationships while on the road can be a nuisance that retirees seek to avoid.

http://time.com/money/3994596/consolidate-retirement-accounts-pay-off/

https://money.usnews.com/investing/investing-101/articles/2018-05-16/5-reasons-to-consolidate-your-investing-accounts

https://www.thebalance.com/consolidate-retirement-accounts-3861993

https://www.forbes.com/sites/financialfinesse/2011/06/17/should-you-consolidate-your-retirement-accounts/#1d1f12c29297

http://www.chicagotribune.com/business/yourmoney/sc-cons-0122-journey-20150119-column.html

Hierarchy of Communication

- During my call center tenure, I shared my write-it-down experiences with a friend who happened to be an anthropology grad student. He surmised that the differing reactions over the phone to my offer to type versus write may stem from writing being part of our genetic and cultural memory. The oldest known pictographs, found in southeast Turkey, are over 12,000 years old. The oldest known cave drawings, as of this writing, were found in Spain and are over 64,000 years old. The typewriter was only invented in 1866. Telling the caller that I was going to type something may not have even registered in their subconscious. Even when sitting across a desk from someone, writing remains more impactful than typing, as a nonverbal maneuver. Typing requires you to break full-body interaction with the customer to interact with your computer instead. Remember, that full-body interaction is a nonverbal maneuver in its own right that conveys you are listening and engaged with the speaker fully.

- In 1971, Carl William Buehner was quoted as saying, "They may forget what you said, but they will never forget how you made them feel." This observation eloquently reinforces non-verbal communication's greater impact relative to verbal communication.

- Written communication can obviously be quite nuanced. Context, ALL CAPS, **bold**, <u>underline</u>, FONT, color, background color, size, etc. all serve to enhance or diminish written communication.

Remember though, if the writing or sign is simply ignored, these visual modifiers also have little to no impact.

- A simple sentence structure technique I learned from my mother enhances the efficacy of your verbal communication. When my mom wanted me to stop doing something, instead of telling me to stop doing that, she would tell me to do what she wanted me to do instead. I cannot recall her ever saying, "Stop doing that," or "Don't do that." She would always tell me to do the thing she wanted me to do. I can still hear her voice saying, "Do this son," or "Do it this way son." "Stand up straight," she would say. "Don't slouch," or "Stop slouching," she would never say. When you speak on purpose, your verbal call to action is the focal point. No energy is given to the negative; all focus is on the desired outcome.

- Many aspects of verbal communication, such as speech modifiers and emotions conveyed, blur the line between verbal and non-verbal communication. Earnestness, sarcasm, regional accent, anger, fear, joy, sincerity, volume, and tone, while being received via the ear, can strengthen or weaken your message's actual words and/or communicate far more information than the words themselves (e.g. – a strong Boston accent may tell a listener you grew up in the Northeast even though your upbringing never came up in conversation.). While I categorize these communication aspects as non-verbal due to their message impact potential, it matters little where you place them in the hierarchy. More importantly, use them on purpose.

- Conference calls are notorious for listeners tuning out. Listeners also commonly report feeling calls are too long or not impactful. Conference calls also provide prime opportunities to speak on purpose.

- While on a conference call recently, I heard the featured speaker provide a lengthy explanation for why her voice was hoarse. She apologized repeatedly before, during and immediately after her phone presentation and even said, "I sound so bad," during her intro. While self-deprecation has its value as a speaking tool in many circumstances, this occasion was not one of them. When speaking on purpose, consider the setting or context and your goal or desired impact. In most presentations, via phone or in person, your goal presumably includes being taken seriously. Were the speaker in this instance speaking on purpose, she may have acknowledged or begged the listeners' pardon for her hoarse voice (which was outside of her control at that point), once, at the outset, and then simply completed her presentation. When your inclination is to verbally self-deprecate (due to nervousness or any other reason), consider the context and your desired impact then ask yourself, "Would the company CEO do this?" Speak on purpose.

- When she was alive, my mother frequently told me, "I can show you better than I can tell you." Another oft-repeated mantra we have all heard is, "Actions speaks louder than words." Clearly the generations that came before ours knew that verbal communication was not the pinnacle of effective communication.

- Speak on purpose using all levels of the hierarchy of communication to engage speakers and listeners effectively on multiple levels.

MODULE 2: Words Matter

When you begin speaking on purpose in earnest, you will often notice those who are not speaking on purpose. Consider the following scenarios.

2.1 Money for Nothing

In a hurry, on your way home from work, you stop at a convenience store to pick up a gallon of milk and a loaf of bread. The label on the shelf below each item reads $2.50. You quickly snag the items and head toward the register to check out. After the cashier scans the items and the $5.00 total appears on the electronic display screen in front of you, the cashier says, "There will be a $5.00 fee." Do you pay the fee?

When this scenario is posed to everyday people, the answer is overwhelmingly and enthusiastically, "No!" Why on Earth would anyone pay a fee to buy groceries? Indeed, many people when faced with this scenario, say they would travel further, to a less convenient store, where milk and bread are $3.00 each, simply to avoid paying a fee.

Why is paying a fee, even a relatively small one, so difficult to accept?

In another scenario, on your way home from work, you stop at a gas station to fill up your full-size SUV. You exit the truck, head toward the pump and do the math (a 30-gallon tank, at nearly $3.00 per gallon, comes to about $90). Do you pump the gas?

When this scenario is posed to everyday people, the answer is overwhelmingly yet despondently, "Yes." In fact, many report this exact scenario playing out in real life. They say they watch the total on the electronic display screen scrolling higher, while remembering paying much less to fill up the same tank only a few years ago. When the pump stops, no one enjoys paying $90.00 for fuel. Everyone knows though, you will not get anywhere on an empty tank. Filling up your SUV will cost you.

Why is paying a cost, even a relatively high one, easier to accept?

Jargon is the phenomenon at play here. Often, jargon acts as an impediment to effective communication between providers of goods and services and their customers. Jargon seeps into everything, quietly, day-to-day. Jargon takes no prisoners. As you might expect, use of jargon is common among those who do not speak on purpose.

As we examine the word fee, we do not ask, "How does Merriam-Webster define fee?" Rather we ask, "What does the word fee mean to businesses? What does the word fee actually mean to everyday people?"

2.2 Keep 'Em Separated

In business, 'fee' is common jargon used to indicate money a client pays in exchange for some valuable good or service the business provides. Sadly (for the business) that meaning is usually lost on everyday people. In practice, the word fee says to the subconscious mind there will be no exchange of value—the precise opposite of what the business intends. When they see or hear the word fee, clients essentially forget the thing of value, even when that thing of value should be obvious. Clients instinctively regard fees as unnecessary virtual cover charges (e.g. – paying for the privilege to buy groceries).

Remember Harry Potter's© invisibility cloak? Using the word fee effectively places an invisibility cloak over a thing of value causing its value to simply vanish into thin air right before a client's eyes.

In the scenario with the milk and bread, the cashier in fact cuts a deal by waiving the taxes. Alas, because the cashier refers to the money being paid in exchange for the milk and bread as a fee, the vast majority of people simply separate the items (the items they came in for, the items right in front of them in a bag ready to go, the items they rationally know are priced at $5.00) from the money requested. This is how the word fee works. Like magic, 'fee' separates a thing from its value, masking the value in the client's mind.

2.3   Value Added

The word 'cost' works the exact opposite way (a counter-spell in magical parlance), subconsciously bringing a thing's value sharper into focus. When a client is being asked to shell out money, the word cost says to the subconscious mind, "You are getting something of value in exchange for your money." 'Cost' prods the mind to seek value out, versus disregarding value when it is otherwise clear. Remarkably, even when a value proposition is not clearly matched to the client need, use of the word cost can prompt the mind to involuntarily scroll through a list of potential needs to match the value proposition. Amazingly, this subconscious search for a value exchange persists, even when the item being evaluated is intangible.

Agent: "Jim, this idea is going to cost you $500.00."

Jim: "I have the money. What's the idea?"

2.4   "Words are things." —Maya Angelou

Words have power. If I want clients to mentally lean away, utterly and subconsciously reject what I propose, and ignore any value I aim to provide—using the word fee is a surefire way to accomplish this goal. On the other hand, if I want clients to mentally lean in and seriously consider what I propose while actively seeking the value I aim to provide—using the word cost is an effective way to do this.

2.5   Jargon Inertia

In spite of everything outlined above, the word fee remains widely used throughout financial services and many other industries. In the financial services industry, there are fee schedules, fee-based advisors, late fees, transfer fees, fee this and fee that. The word fee is everywhere! Why? Call it *jargon inertia*. Jargon Inertia exists because jargon is an integral component of any industry culture, including yours. Even when we are harmed by the use of jargon, we continue to use it.

Customers demand fee waivers so frequently these days that waivers are beginning to add up. Many financial institutions now actively track fee waivers at the branch level. Some even account for them on their corporate financial statements, offsetting the fee income included in their non-interest income. Why are customers demanding to waive fees? In the context of what is outlined in this book, they are not connecting the value of some service being provided by the bank to the money coming out of their account in exchange for that service.

Consider the following Overdraft Fee interaction:

Teller: "Dan, you didn't have enough money in your account, so—as agreed—we went ahead and paid that bill for you. The cost was $36.00."

Dan: "Okay, thanks."

Now consider the following Stop Payment Fee interaction:

Banker: "Bob, you wrote a check to this, um, ah, 'business,' and you're saying you don't want the check to clear and show up on the statement which your wife sees, right? Alright, we're going to arrange that. That service will cost you $36.00."

Bob: "Okay, thanks."

If this were how tellers and bankers were trained to interact with customers, fee waivers would decline...drastically. Why? People do not ask to waive costs! That would be asking to get something for free and by and large people do not behave this way in professional settings. Humans tend to exhibit an innate sense of fairness and are generally willing to pay a reasonable cost for something from which they receive equitable value. It would be even better for the banking industry if the Overdraft and Stop Payment Fees were labeled Overdraft & Stop Payment Costs on customer statements. I posit that such a change would actually prevent a sizeable number of fee-related arguments in the branch and over the phone.

Upon reading the previous paragraph, a skeptic may say, "Of course clients get it. It's outlined in the Fee Schedule when they open the account. People are asking for something for free when they ask to waive a fee."

I would respond to the skeptic by saying, "People hate the word fee so much, many would physically attack your tellers if we lived in a less civilized society. Customers are not asking to receive something for free when they ask to waive a fee; they are asking you to stop taking their money and throwing it down a black hole, which is a metaphor for taking their money and providing no value in exchange."

If you are relying solely on your written Fee Schedule to handle the subconscious disconnect between service providers and customers I have outlined, I am truly sorry for you. It does not and will not work, as evidenced by the fact that nearly every financial institution publishes a regularly updated fee schedule and said schedule has no discernible impact on fee waiver requests. Anything communicated in a fee schedule is dead-on-arrival as a means of connecting your value to the money leaving your customer's account. Besides, you should not be relying on written communication solely anyway. See Module 1.

'Fee' is a powerful word and we have been blind to its power in our industry. Some jargon is simply confusing to people outside the industry associated with that jargon. Other jargon is actually dangerous because it has a translation in plain English that means something completely different than how its industry defines it. 'Fee' is dangerous jargon.

What can you do? Speak on purpose.

I know avoiding jargon is difficult, due in large part to jargon inertia. Follow the steps laid out in this book. Speaking on purpose, including jargon avoidance, will become considerably less difficult. No human is perfect. I train people to speak on purpose and I still find myself using the word fee occasionally. In fact, I am self-conscious about it! Nevertheless, when you discipline yourself to speak on purpose, you will find the results begin to speak for themselves. No pun intended.

2.6   Making Change

If you are particularly forward thinking, and responsible for your organization's literature, change your verbiage in writing. Replace 'fee' with 'cost' in all of your documents when there is in fact some service or value being provided in exchange for money leaving a customer's account. When publishing your Cost Schedule, clearly outline the value or service being provided in exchange.

I have trained dozens of banks and hundreds of bank employees in eight states on this concept to one degree or another. I am still waiting to see my first Cost Schedule, which is an excellent example of how powerful jargon inertia can be. We often know what to do and why we should do it. Yet we simply continue doing what we have been doing. Failure becomes the norm, comfortable even.

From time to time an observant lender will point out that lenders use the word cost and therefore must grasp this concept already. I simply point out that the term Closing Costs is likely used because it is an alliteration that rolls off the tongue easily. Until the Loan Origination Fee becomes the Loan Origination Cost and all other assorted fees in the loan process are replaced by costs, lenders—like everyone else in the financial services industry—should endeavor to speak on purpose.

2.7   Products Solve Nothing

The smart phone that you used to call/text/read/play games on earlier today likely came over to the USA on a boat from China. If so, while being shipped on that boat it sat in a container along with millions of its brethren. That phone is a product. Period. Full stop.

When you purchased it, activated it and began using it, it became a solution to a problem, namely your need to call, text, read and play games.

Consider the impact if you were to speak on purpose and consistently refer to the items you are proposing to clients as solutions or even potential solutions. (Hello compliance departments!) The impact on the client subconscious could be profound.

Products are simply things in the subconscious mind, things that are not connected to value or even to clients themselves. Product in plain English is not jargon, but it is not much of anything else.

Solution on the other hand, is a word that subconsciously implies there is a problem and what you propose may be the answer to it. Again, even if the problem is intangible or difficult to define, 'solution' prompts the subconscious mind to begin looking for the connection. Is this not precisely what you want your client to do? To actually listen to your proposal and consider it?

When institutions and individuals use the word product, they make it more difficult on themselves. Use of the term product forces the service provider to do most of the heavy lifting in the effort to connect the dots between value and client. Doable certainly, but using the word solution provides a helpful boost to your efforts because it activates the client's subconscious search engine. Now with the client searching for value and the provider seeking to provide value, it is far more likely the client and provider work together to connect the dots. Connections reached this way are often stronger in nature. Speak on purpose.

2.8 Defer Jargon Indefinitely

Have you ever visited a fast food restaurant and heard a cashier offer to super-size an order or upgrade it in some way? If so, have you ever heard this response, "Thank you, but I'll defer." Probably not. Why? People do not use the words defer or deferral in casual common speech. In the financial services industry though, you may hear the word regularly. Certainly 'defer' and 'deferral' (as in tax-deferral) are only mild jargon words that are easily explained. Nonetheless, when you speak on purpose, aim to prevent confusion resulting from jargon, mild or otherwise.

'Tax-Shelter' is a term that can evoke images of rich people, often celebrities and business tycoons, hiding their money from Uncle Sam. These images may inspire anger in some or envy in others. Regardless, many folks wish they had enough money to desperately want to hide it from Uncle Sam.

When you describe a tax-deferred instrument (e.g. – IRAs, HSAs, etc.) in this fashion, it can help your client begin his or her journey toward actual understanding. "An Individual Retirement Account is a legal tax-shelter everyday people can use to grow their money larger and faster because money is not taxed while it is inside the account. More growth may mean more golf or groceries later in life." When speaking on purpose, using words that evoke images (e.g. – golf, groceries) often makes your presentation more effective.

2.9   Just Stop

It is not only jargon that stops us from expressing ourselves more effectively. Some words are not jargon at all and they still misconstrue our meaning inadvertently.

You may begin some of your client calls with, "Hi, I'm just calling to touch base." Stop doing that. First, 'touching base,' 'following up,' 'reaching out' and 'catching up' are all blather, or words with no substance. Blather is worse than jargon, especially when coming from someone we do not want to hear from. Second, by placing the word just in front of what you are calling about, anything you are calling about has subconsciously been labeled irrelevant in advance...by you. While use of 'just' in this particular context is often designed to convey a lack of difficulty or complexity, it is not precise enough in its conveyance. When using 'just,' you inadvertently include and emphasize the normally undesired overtone of a lack of importance. An alternative to 'just' is 'simply.' "I'm simply calling to share an idea that I believe you'll like." 'Simply' specifically implies that what follows is simple, not difficult or complex. 'Just' implies first and foremost that what follows is unimportant. This is a subtle, yet powerful distinction. Speak on purpose.

2.10 So Far So Good, But...

"I really like that outfit you're wearing today Tom, but..."

What just happened? Everything I said before the word but was negated—completely. Anything said prior to 'but' is irrelevant. 'But,' when used in this particular context, is the fulcrum of the sentence, set firmly between what is unimportant and what is important. Usually a listener only wants to hear what is important. Any goodwill built up prior to the word but is exhausted immediately upon utterance of this unassuming, single-syllable, three-letter word.

What to do? It may be awkward sometimes, but consider using the word 'and' when possible. In the previous sentence, note that I use 'but' to my advantage. I specifically wanted to minimize the preceding phrase on awkwardness. I spoke on purpose.

"I really like that outfit you're wearing today Tom, and I'm upset that you're late."

When we use 'and' as the fulcrum of the sentence we avoid the summary execution of every word that came beforehand. This is another subtle, yet powerful distinction when communicating. In the previous sentence, note that 'yet' is not quite as brutal as 'but' in its effect on the preceding words, even though it is an essentially synonymous conjunction. In fact, when 'yet' is used as an adverb it can even evoke hope. When compared to 'but,' similar conjunctions (though, although, etc.) are all far less powerful in minimizing their preceding phrase. 'And,' is a conjunction that is not synonymous with 'but' in any way. As a result, when you use 'and' instead of 'but,' remember mild awkwardness may ensue. Awkwardness may be a small price to pay to avoid invalidating entire fragments of your sentence.

'Fee,' 'product,' 'just' and 'but' are a very small sampling of the many words, both jargon and common, that can impact a listener's subconscious in unexpected and undesired ways. Jargon often leaves a listener confused. Blather often leaves them bored. TED Speaker Jason Fried says, "Jargon is insecurity. Instead of using strong, clear, words that accurately reflect concepts, we lapse into vague corporate speak by parroting beaten-to-death jargon" (Cullen, 2018). Bottom line? You want the client to listen, understand and consider your proposal? Speaking on purpose moves the conversation toward this goal more effectively than not doing so. Take control of your verbiage to have the desired impact on your listener. Speak on purpose.

2.11 Reflections on Module 2

"The young man knows the rules. The old man knows the exceptions."

–Oliver Wendell Holmes

When do you use the words I have trained you not to use? When speaking on purpose!

- When do you say 'fee?' When you are referencing a competitor and would like to saddle that competitor with the subconscious no-value image 'fee' invokes. "I've heard many complaints about the fees at AAA Bank. It's sad. Here at BBB Credit Union our members prefer our low-cost approach."

- When do you say 'product?' When discussing what your competitors offer. "You mentioned CCC. While their product is featured in a radio commercial, the DDD solution is best suited to the specific issues we've outlined here."

- When do you say 'tax-deferral?' As is the case with most jargon, use it when you want the person you are speaking with to be mildly confused.

- When do you say 'just?' When you specifically want to minimize whatever follows. "It's alright Joe, just take a sip. It'll be fine."

- When do you say 'but?' When you want to minimize or eliminate whatever came before. "I know it seems hard but it is actually pretty easy."

- Overcoming Objections is a common sales training topic. Consider the non-verbal imagery that phrase evokes. What customer wants to be overcome? Speak on purpose. Embrace Objections instead. Most people like hugs. Repeat objections back to the customer to confirm you heard it the way they meant it. Acknowledge that you understand and appreciate their concerns. Then go about outlining how you plan to address their concerns. That may have been your process already. How you refer to it matters though. Words matter. You are a customer in some form nearly every day. Given a choice, would you or any customer rather be overcome or embraced?

- There are many words—jargon and non-jargon alike—that we can change in speech and writing. 'Think' and 'thought' become 'believe' and 'belief,' as appropriate. Compared to 'think,' 'believe' evokes more conviction and passion, for instance.

- Turn passive phrases into active phrases. Active phrases also convey more conviction and passion. If you choose to be less direct, so be it. Do it on purpose though!
  - "Give me a call," becomes "Call me."
  - "Feel free to call me," becomes "Call me."
  - "Have a nice day," becomes "Make it a great day."
  - "Um" and "Uh" are words too! They convey lack of preparation. Do not use them.

- Words can often be placed on the **grid of impact/connation** (*see figure 3*). Depending on context and usage, move your verbiage from left to right as best you can. Test them for yourself.

Grid of Impact/Connation		
Negative	Neutral	Positive
Fee		Cost
	Product	Solution

Grid of Impact/Connation		
Negative	Neutral	Positive
Just	Simply	
But	And	
	Think	Believe
Cheap	Inexpensive	
I'm Good		Thank You
Unfortunately	Actually	
	Free	Complimentary
No		Yes
Overcome		Embrace
	Tax-Defer	Tax-Shelter
	Business	Practice
	Lead	Opportunity
Ask		Invite
	Dude/Man/Bud	Sir
Sell		Help

Figure 3

- Do you own your own financial services business or do you own your own financial services practice? The word practice subconsciously evokes a higher level of professionalism and gravitas. Doctors, lawyers and accountants appear to have that figured out. Speak on purpose.

- Have you ever held an event and wanted people to attend? In this context, when you ask someone to attend, you connote (whether you realize it or not) that they are helping you. When you invite them to attend, you connote that you are helping them. Which connotation do you believe will drive greater attendance? Speak on purpose.

- When speaking to customers, clients, fellow professionals or anyone, consider replacing generic nouns such as dude, man, bro, buddy and bud with their more respectful counterpart, sir. 'Sir' denotes respect and need not be reserved solely for those in authority or with seniority. Nearly any interaction, business or personal, will be rendered more effective with a purposeful extra helping of respect.

- Sales professionals the world over know that purposefully avoiding words that trigger instant negative reactions, allows the customer to remain focused on the information being presented. This focus further allows the customer to consider the information in light of their situation and ultimately make a fully informed and thoughtful decision, whether the decision is yes or no. There is precisely zero value in receiving an inadvertently triggered, instant negative response based on word usage, especially when compared to a thoughtful yet informative negative response based the merits of what is being presented. Far too many customers are demonstrably harmed by not even hearing the solution to their problem because some word or phrase triggered a knee-jerk negative reaction. Speaking on purpose seeks to ensure customers are actually receiving potentially helpful information, versus useless information, no information or harmful information.

MODULE 3: The Referral Scale

It is common practice for employees to receive referral training in banks, credit unions and many other business settings. Nearly all financial institution staff worldwide (from teller to executive) have gone through numerous, expensive and often lengthy training sessions on referrals. Whether we are being trained to refer customers to the lending, credit card, investment, or some other department, referral training has become ubiquitous.

In spite of this, it remains an oft-heard mantra amongst the folks who seek to receive referrals that they are not receiving enough of them. When referrals are brought up the blame game can go into overtime and the label maker can come out in full force, as the person or persons not receiving referrals judges the staff members who are not providing them as lazy, disinterested, etc. At the core of this issue is, as a man I respect named Rob Dearman puts it, a "five letter word that starts with t...trust." More on that later.

First, let's identify each level on "The Referral Scale" and ensure you are aiming for the precise outcome you desire at your institution.

3.1   Absolutely Nothing, Say It Again

Imagine you are walking into a newly built, neighborhood big box store for the first time and in a hurry. You are looking for a hammer, having misplaced yours. As you stand near the front of the store, you crane your neck in an effort to read the signs or spot the tool section, but to no avail. At some point you become aware of a young man stocking shelves nearby and, as you look toward him, he actually turns and looks toward you. You both make eye contact. You believe it is quite clear to anyone looking at you that you are in search of something in the store. After a moment of eye contact, the stock boy turns away and continues to stock his shelves.

Pause.

Think about how the stock boy's response makes you feel. Not good, I suspect. I have heard several emotions described by trainees when presented with this scenario: anger, embarrassment, sadness and others—all negative. We call a customer service experience like that 'nothing' because no service was given. So on the referral scale, we define an outrageously poor, worthless and ineffectual customer service experience as 'nothing.' Any casual observer would likely agree that in this context, 'nothing' is—to use a technical term—crap. Remember this.

3.2   The Elusive Referral

Let's go back to the imagined scenario in the big-box store where you are looking for a new hammer in a hurry. In this version, upon making eye contact the stock boy immediately smiles and asks, "May I help you?" You explain that you are looking for a hammer, and the smiling stock boy says, "Certainly. You're very close. Walk down two aisles to your right, then turn left. Half way down that aisle, there'll be a big sign that says hammers and you'll see them all. You can't miss them."

You take off following those directions and, lo and behold, you find the hammers, pick one and head toward the register. That worked great!

Generally speaking, we can all agree that was a vastly better customer service experience. The stock boy spoke clearly and gave detailed, accurate directions that worked perfectly. You were in a hurry so his succinct response was appreciated as well. A customer service experience like that is called a 'referral' on our scale, and to be crystal clear, most businesses absolutely love referrals. They can be hard to come by, elusive even, which is why businesses spend so much time and money training on them. Furthermore, a 'referral' experience is orders of magnitude better than a 'nothing' experience from the customer's perspective.

3.3   Better Than a Referral?

Alright, you are back in the aforementioned scenario, at the store looking for a hammer in a hurry. The stock boy engages, asking if he can help. You say you are looking for a hammer and he smiles, stops what he is doing, then walks toward you saying, "I'll show you!" He then proceeds to escort you to the nearby hammer section. Once you begin perusing the selection, he confirms that you are all set and goes back to his work station to finish stocking shelves.

Have you ever had an actual experience like that in a store? How did that make you feel? Much better than the 'nothing' experience and at least a little better than the 'referral' experience, right? It was not absolutely necessary for the stock boy to stop what he was doing and escort you. The hammer section was very close. Nonetheless, that small gesture had an outsized impact on how you felt as a customer, in the moment. We call that type of customer service experience an 'introduction' on our scale. And while a 'referral' is far-and-away a better customer service experience than "nothing," on the referral scale an 'introduction' is better still.

3.4   Aim High

If your branch or institution already excels at referrals, start aiming them higher up the scale, toward introductions. What might a referral look like in the bank versus the big-box store? In your branch, after helping a customer make a deposit, you ask a question. Something as simple as, "Have you met Lorie, our Financial Planner?" You follow that up by handing Lorie's business card to the intrigued customer as a referral. Asking that same question after you have helped the customer with a deposit, then walking them over to Lorie's desk to introduce him or her to Lorie is an introduction.

3.5   Reach The Top

We started this module at the bottom of the referral scale with 'nothing.' Our scale has one last entry, at the very top. One last time, we now revisit our scenario at the beginning, in the big-box store, looking for a hammer in a hurry. The stock boy engages you, asks to help, escorts you over to the hammers, and then says, "These Stanley® hammers are on sale." or "My dad always used Craftsman® hammers, they're great quality tools."

What just happened? Will the stock boy receive a 50 cent referral bonus from Stanley® for mentioning their brand name? Not likely. Does he have a Craftsman® quota? Specifically, is he responsible for unloading the store's brand-specific hammer inventory on customers? Doubtful. This customer service experience, far rarer than the 'introduction,' is called an 'endorsement' on the referral scale. The endorsement sits at the peak of our scale and should be our ultimate goal in both training & execution. The stock boy was not motivated by incentives or quotas (carrots or sticks). He simply wanted to help the customer. In this case by providing some simple, helpful information related to the customer's search. Now that is service and not crap, any casual observer would likely agree.

3.6   Aim Higher

Aim your branch or institution at the top of the scale. Train them to make endorsements. This is an example of speaking on purpose in your training efforts. By designing your trainings as Referral Trainings, referrals are what you can expect if all goes according to plan. If the plan fails, you will likely get nothing at your institution. Aiming toward introductions, may result in referrals and aiming at endorsements may result in introductions. Train on purpose.

3.7   Hurry Up

Remember, as you began each experience, you were in a hurry. The nothing got you nothing. The referral got you what you needed. The introduction got you what you needed and made you feel better about the experience. The endorsement got you what you needed, made you feel better about the experience, and helped you understand the solution being offered a little better. Importantly, these significantly different service experiences did not take substantially more time to complete when compared to one another. In reality, the endorsement experience may have cost you, the customer, less time. The endorsement experience directed you toward the hammer and provided an answer, in advance, to a couple of common hammer questions. The nothing experience forced you to waste time searching and (if you ever even found the hammers) waste time wondering which hammer was best or on sale.

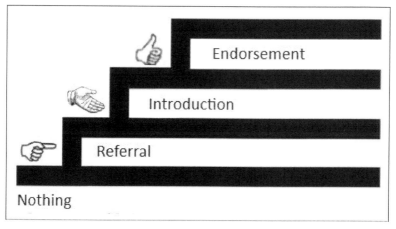

Figure 4

Whichever service experience you choose to provide your customer from this scale (*see figure 4*) choose and provide that experience on purpose.

3.8   Reflections on Module 3

- What is the most common question heard in banks nationwide, after helping a customer with some mundane transaction? "Is there anything else I can help you with?" This is unfortunate, because that question is effectively a nothing experience to customers and we earlier established that nothing is crap…technically speaking. There are many reasons that question qualifies as nothing. Below are a few:

o There is nearly zero potential to add value to the customer experience with that question. The answer is nearly universally, "No." The primary value-add of the teller completing the transaction has come and gone. That question does not provide any potentially helpful information.

o Often, even the employee asking the question knows it is a throw-away question. The question is simply borne of habit and asked as part of a routine designed to move the customer along. The customer knows the routine and answers accordingly. (Just like people greeting each other with, "What's up?" They commonly do not care what's up or even answer the question. It is routine.)

o Once in a blue moon, a client will remember something else they need help with. Great. By asking "Is there anything else I can help you with?" you place the burden on the customer to recall their heretofore forgotten need. Is your value proposition truly that you jog people's memory? What if the customer does not know (despite all the signage) that your institution can help with the other thing on her mind but you actually can? She will not mention her need to you! Do everyone a favor, do not ask nothing questions. Be specific and ask questions related to the value-added services your institution provides.

- Endorsement experiences must be based on truth. If the Stanley® hammers are not actually on sale, the customer service experience will go south fast once the customer reaches the cash register. If the banker gives an endorsement by saying, "Let me introduce you to Jeff, our Financial Planner. He helped me with my retirement plan," then Jeff better have actually helped the banker with his retirement plan.

- Remember the five letter word that starts with t? Folks who seek to receive referrals, introductions or endorsements from the staff members who are ostensibly tasked with providing them must engender trust with those staff members. If the staff members do not inherently and unequivocally trust the people to whom they are tasked with referring to, they simply never will. Financial Planners who spend some time building rapport with the staff, or actually discussing the bank's 401(k) plan with staff members privately in an office, will directly impact their referral volume. Mortgage Lenders who offer to answer questions about staff members own mortgages or home owning aspirations will directly impact their referral volume. If you want to receive referrals, introductions or endorsements, begin by fostering trust to make your team more comfortable with breaking the nothing question routine.

MODULE 4: Ask On Purpose

In Module 3, we reflected on why the question, "Is there anything else I can help you with?" is a 'nothing' question. In this module, we will further examine this question and others.

4.1   Transactional Energy Imbalance

In human interactions, when we help one another in some way, energy is exchanged. The helper has given and the person helped has received, which may result in an imbalance. In anthropology, psychology and other scientific disciplines, this phenomenon is explored in great detail by studies on so-called honor cultures or face cultures. In truth, this type of energy exchange and resulting imbalance exists to some degree in nearly all human interaction, regardless of culture. When an imbalance is created, while completely subconscious, it can greatly influence the behavior of both parties going forward.

The degree of the imbalance directly relates to the nature of the help, as perceived by the person being helped. If you stop to help someone fix a flat tire, on a dark road, in the cold, in the rain, in the middle of nowhere, after a dozen other cars have driven by without stopping, you have helped a lot. If you take someone's order at a cash register, you have helped a little.

In the case of the flat tire, the many circumstances combine to ensure that the person you are helping consciously recognizes how incredibly valuable your help is. In the case of the cash register transaction, you are simply doing your job, the job you are expected to do. You are not going above-and-beyond the call of duty—the call-of-duty simply being your job description.

Of course, you could always, in spite of the consequences, choose not to do your job at the cash register (i.e. - ignore the customer, get the order wrong, be rude, etc.). Subconsciously at least, customers know this. Therefore, when you simply do your job you are still recognized by the customer as being helpful, simply less so when compared to changing a flat tire in the rain and more subconsciously than consciously. In either scenario a *transactional energy imbalance* may be created.

4.2   Balance Restoration Ritual

With this in mind, consider transactions at the teller line. Customers are often in a hurry to complete their business. Oftentimes they stand in long lines before reaching the teller window, which can make them even more anxious to simply finish making their deposit, withdrawal, etc. Despite the need for speed and potential anxiety, after we help them complete these relatively mundane tasks listed in our job description, we nearly always ask them one more question. We do not even need to be trained to do so. Why do we nearly always ask a question? Again, it is transactional energy imbalance. Both parties feel it, both parties abhor it and all of us humans have instinctively developed a neat little ritual to restore balance. Our balance restoration ritual is the question and the answer.

Here is how the ritual works. After we help the bank customer we subconsciously sense the imbalance. We then provide the customer an opportunity to restore balance by asking a question. "Is there anything else I can help you with?" The customer also senses the imbalance and, consequently, answers our question (often happily), restoring the balance, "Nope, all set. Thanks." In the bank transaction scenario, the person helping initiates the ritual.

After we help the person with the flat tire, the person is extremely likely to ask us to accept some money or other compensation in order to repay the perceived debt (imbalance). They will even insist if we refuse because the imbalance is significant in this scenario. Again, both parties in a helpful interaction feel the imbalance, dislike it, and ordinarily seek to restore balance. In the flat tire scenario, the person being helped initiates the ritual.

If you are the teller providing help and you are speaking on purpose, you are asking the naturally occurring ritual question on purpose. Instead of nothing questions, you are asking a question that has more potential to help the customer further. Regardless of whether you ask a helpful question or a nothing question, once the customer gives their answer, balance is restored and your opportunity to provide more help ends.

By fully comprehending the transactional energy imbalance stemming from nearly any customer interaction, you will better grasp that the resultant balance restoration ritual represents a golden opportunity. Whether your branch conducts 50 or 50,000 transactions per day, each transaction is an opportunity to ask a potentially helpful question instead of a nothing question. Understanding transactional energy imbalance and the balance restoration ritual also reminds us that the person being asked a question subconsciously wants to answer it.

4.3   Hijack The Ritual

As you seek to actually help customers and restore balance, consider hijacking the ritual by hijacking nothing questions. When you simply do your job, you earn the right to ask nearly any simple question. Hijack the ritual and ask questions that, while simple, contain true potential to meaningfully help. Meaningful questions from the teller or banker may include:

- o Want zero interest on your credit cards?
- o Want to cut your mortgage in half?
- o Have you met our consumer lender?
- o Have you met our personal banker?

o Have you met our branch manager?

o Have you met our financial planner?

o Have you met Robb? (Where Robb works in any of the previous 4 roles)

o Do you like paying taxes?

These are questions that can result in someone else who works at the bank actually helping the customer, if the customer responds accordingly. If the customer does not respond accordingly, balance is still restored, the opportunity has ended and the ritual is complete. All of which is status quo when compared to nothing questions. At some point after every transaction, the balance will usually be restored and the opportunity to help further will end. Seek to reach this point on purpose while also trying to actually help your customers. Avoid reaching this point through habit, without conscious thought and without any significant potential to help anyone.

4.4   Reflections on Helpful Questions

- As I write this, the average US credit card APR has hit a record high, 17.55%. Also, US credit card debt in the US has surpassed $1 trillion, its highest level ever, even higher than just before or during the Great Recession. Finally, Americans paid over $104 billion in credit card interest and fees in 2017, up 11% from 2016 and up 35% from 2012. Balance transfers frequently provide zero interest for a period of six-to-twelve months. That reduction in interest can be very helpful to customers holding a credit card balance at a high rate. We are not promising to provide zero interest, as that would obviously depend upon whether the customer is approved or not. We are simply asking if zero interest is something the customer would like, in an effort to help further. (*Source: creditcards.com. CNBC, Federal Reserve, Marketwatch*)

https://www.creditcards.com/credit-card-news/rate-report.php

https://www.cnbc.com/2018/01/23/credit-card-debt-hits-record-high.html

- One of the basic ideas behind a mortgage refinance is lowering the original mortgage payment. Again, we are not promising to lower their payment or even cut it in half, that would depend on their refinance application. We are asking if lowering a mortgage payment is something the customer would like. We never get to the application to find out if it is possible if we do not ask the initial question.

- Many customers have never met the planner, lender, banker or manager. Ostensibly, each of these individuals can actually help a customer further in some form, now or later. Certainly if any of these bank employees have been recently hired, this question adds value, simply by ensuring the customer is aware that these roles are filled at the bank.

- Many people regularly seek to legally avoid paying taxes. Financial planners at the bank provide an array of helpful strategies to minimize tax burdens for clients.

- The questions in section 4.3 are only a few of the many potentially helpful questions that can be asked post-transaction at the teller line or at the banker's desk. Each question is an example of how simple it is for the financial institution employee to hijack nothing questions to ask helpful questions instead.

4.5   CEO Questions

Generally speaking, after helping the customer with a simple transaction, you have only earned the right to ask simple questions not complex ones. Questions should be eight words or less (more on this later). Questions should not be open-ended, contrary to sales training you may have been provided. I have received much of that training myself over the years and I am stating this unequivocally, open-ended questions are wrong for the teller line. A simple teller transaction does not generate a transactional energy imbalance large enough to warrant an open-ended question.

In the teller setting, I suggest you ask what I call "closed end optional" questions or CEO questions. CEO questions are closed-end yes-or-no questions that provide the customer with a clear option to 'open' the end of the question with more detail or follow up questions. CEO questions allow the customer to delve deeper if the question piques their interest. They also allow the customer to keep the question closed and get on with their day if the question does not pique their interest sufficiently, in the moment. Since the 'option to open' belongs to the customer, there is no pressure on the teller to 'find a need.' If a CEO question sparks interest, it will be clear right away. If it does not, the teller gave it a sincere effort with a potentially helpful question versus a nothing question.

Pure open-ended questions are seldom appropriate in a teller-transaction setting, which is often too fast-paced and public. Tellers inherently know this and frequently refuse to ask open-ended questions, even when instructed to do so. Clients usually do not want to provide their life story at the teller line and tellers do not feel comfortable asking them to do so.

Bankers have more leeway, as they are often sitting at a desk, more deeply engaged with at least a modicum of privacy. Bankers are welcome to ask open-end questions as appropriate. The power of CEO questions should not be forgotten, however, even in the banker setting. Bankers generally ask open-ended questions while they are exploring a subject that has already been broached. The CEO question is designed to broach a new subject while empowering the client to determine if the new subject will be explored at all.

Remember that you have earned the right to ask these simple yet potentially helpful questions. How did you earn that right? You helped the client. Notice the verb is 'helped' not "helping." Until the client has been fully helped to resolution with the item(s) he or she came in to address, you have not earned the right to ask anything.

I cannot overstate this aspect of the customer-provider relationship. I frequently encounter bankers asking potentially helpful questions during some natural lull in the primary discussion (the banker's computer froze during loan data entry, the banker is walking the client back to the safe deposit box area, the banker is awaiting an answer from a third party before she can proceed, etc.). In each case, bankers sometimes choose that moment to inquire about something off-topic, though potentially helpful. Since the primary purpose of the interaction has not been addressed, these questions—however well designed or provocative—often result in a negative response. Regardless of the circumstances, if a lull occurs, stay focused on the client's primary purpose. Only upon completion of it, or the completion stage that can be achieved during that visit, have you earned the right to ask anything.

For new employees or individuals who seem unable to implement the strategies outlined in this module, despite them being trained to do so and held accountable for doing so, consider introducing an even simpler process. Nearly every teller window and banker desk I have ever seen contains a bowl of candy or lollipops or something similar. If someone on your team will not ask the helpful questions introduced in this book or questions created in your branch or at your institution, have them ask each client after helping them, "Would you like a piece of candy?" That is another CEO question. Clients will respond yes or no and can absolutely engage with the team member in more detail about the candy if they would like to learn more.

This exercise will demonstrate that candy dishes will empty faster when this question is asked than when it is not. This in turn will highlight the efficacy of using your earned question to add more value and help. How does candy add value or help? It is a tasty treat!

This exercise will also highlight how written communication—the clearly visible presence of a bowl of candy at eye level—pales in comparison to verbal communication. Verbally asking the customer if they would like a piece of candy draws attention to the candy more effectively than carefully placing it in clear view. Many of the people who accept the candy will be regulars who have never asked nor helped themselves to a piece of candy. They simply had not consciously seen or noticed it before.

Simply ask! Ask on purpose. It is not difficult. Ask a question with the potential to help substantively. You have earned it and if you pique someone's interest and ask a question that truly helps that person now or later, he or she will thank you for it, now or later.

4.6   Mickey D's

There is a commonly shared, though possibly apocryphal, story about McDonald's® in the 1980s having great success selling apple pies because they brought their apple pies to the attention of more customers. According to the story they implemented a strategy requiring their employees to ask, "Would you like an apple pie with that?" The question would be asked after they helped each customer with an order. Two principles of the story we have already covered in Module 4. Ask CEO questions (customers were welcome to ask the cashier about sugar content & calories if they wanted more detail) and help first, then ask.

There are other important sales concepts highlighted in this story. McDonald's® in the 1980's was a place many people were already visiting to purchase one thing or another (I certainly visited often). As a result, the question campaign was less about 'selling' apple pies and more about 'informing' customers that apple pies were on the menu. People visiting financial institutions are usually already customers, there is no need to be pushy. The story highlights the fact that 'asking to inform' is not a pushy approach. Helpful questions you earn the right to ask in the bank setting are also less about selling customers additional services and more about informing customers that these helpful services and potential solutions are on the menu.

The story also highlights that, while customers' interest may not be piqued immediately, repeatedly planting seeds of helpful information now, may yield fruit later. Many customers did not want an apple pie at the point-of-sale, nonetheless they became more fully aware that apple pies were a menu item. If they later developed a taste for pie, they knew where to go because of the question. Helpful bank services are often purchased during return visits after information provided in the past has become relevant in the present. If your institution asks helpful questions that do not apply at the moment, when they do apply the customers are more likely to think of your institution first.

Harkening back to Module 1, we know there were apple pie signs throughout the store, but the question from the cashier highlighted the apple pie at the point-of-sale, far more effectively than any signage. There were certainly billboards and commercials promoting the apple pie. There probably would have been people dressed in ridiculous pie costumes dancing on the corner, if McDonald's ® had been more forward thinking back then.

Also note that the question was asked of everyone. McDonald's® did not allow its employees to discriminate via questioning. If employees were told to ask only certain groups of people, inevitably someone from another group—someone who may enjoy a pie—would be missed. If you only ask questions of people with sizeable balances on your customer profile screen, you are missing the people with sizeable balances at other institutions. Indeed, that type of treatment may be why their balance is so small at your bank.

4.7 Eight Words or Less

Finally, notice that "Would you like an apple pie with that?" consists of eight words. This formula works well as it flows and lends itself to a simple question earned after a simple transaction. Any more words and the customer may be confused, the teller may have a hard time remembering the question and you are probably back to square one. As you develop your own questions—for your institution, for your branch or simply for yourself—follow this eight-words-or-less guideline for success. "Would you like a piece of candy?" follows the guideline. Every question in section 4.3 follows the guideline. Definitely make the questions your own. Practice them until they flow off your tongue smoothly. Then ask one of your questions, after you have helped, every time, on purpose.

4.8 Reflections on Module 4

- Often, a teller or banker I am training expresses some degree of anxiety as a result of being asked to adopt a new role (helpful customer advocate versus polite transaction processor). Consider. When we go to school (from elementary to post-graduate) the 'social contract' states that we have simply earned the right to go learn. When we go to school, in principle, our anxiety related to learning should be minimal at best. As a currently employed bank professional, you have earned the right to learn how to be particularly good at helping people. Approach the new concepts outlined in this book as part of an ongoing learning experience. Give yourself permission to try-and-fail, just like students try-and-fail when reading and studying in their efforts to master the subject matter to the best of their ability. Do all of this on purpose.

- Fear of rejection is a common anxiety and bank employees are as susceptible to it as anyone else. No one likes to be told "No." Depending on how the "No" is given, the person it is directed toward can feel belittled, humiliated or both. If fear of being told "No" seems like an obstacle to implementing some of the strategies outlined in Module 4, read on.

- Consider a man who considers himself 'God's gift to women.' When faced with rejection by the women he pursues, he is unfazed. Sometimes he persists. Other times he simply moves on, telling the woman, "It's your loss." While nothing about this individual's behavior should be emulated, we can learn something useful from his mindset.

- In this individual's mind and heart (his true self), he considers his overtures to women as a means of helping those women. I know it sounds absurd, but consider it. When you are asking questions purely as a means of helping customers, if those customers choose not to be helped why would you feel rejected? You would not!

- The negative feelings associated with rejection normally result from the rejected person wanting something to happen that is not happening. When the desired outcome does not occur, the feeling of rejection springs up. If you are asking questions solely in an effort to help customers versus trying to hit your scorecard metrics or snag a referral bonus, rejection will have little impact on you. No one minds when customers respond to, "Is there anything else?" with rejection. No one at McDonald's® was heartbroken if a customer did not want an apple pie. Develop a strong conviction that you are asking questions solely to help. If the answer is no or the CEO question remains closed, you will be fine.

- One more point on CEO questions. As mentioned previously, the option to open the question belongs to the customer. This is particularly important because the customer has the power, they can often feel it and we want them to. When the customer feels that they are no longer in control of their interaction, nearly all of their answers become "No," and their impression of your institution declines rapidly.

- Contrary to some training philosophies, you should want the customer to have the power. The Speak On Purpose training program is specifically designed to ultimately empower the customer. Banks are not used car lots where the teller is trying to sell someone a lemon. Any training designed to trick or pressure the customer always fails in the end and hurts everyone. Employees and customers alike despise such tactics. Note: No offense is directed toward hard-working pre-owned-vehicle sales professionals who help their customers the right way and often speak on purpose in their own right. Sadly, pop culture provides poorly run used car lots as an example of the wrong way to sell, that many people will recognize.

MODULE 5: Implement On Purpose

Financial institutions of any kind are often characterized as conservative in their management approach. In fact, conservatism as it relates to money management is ordinarily a badge of honor in the minds of both employees and customers, and rightly so. As a rule, no one wants their financial institution playing wild and loose with the money.

5.1 Top-Down vs. Bottom-Up

One side-effect of the historically conservative organizational structure found in most financial institutions is a firm reliance on top-down implementation of new ideas. Furthermore, there may be structural barriers (real or perceived) which front line employees must overcome, if they want to share an idea upstream. Admittedly this structure can work, as those who actually overcome upstream barriers to innovate anyway often become the institution's next generation of leaders. Nonetheless, when compared to the rapid innovation seen in many other industries, financial institutions can lag behind.

In technology, manufacturing, marketing and other industries, competition is certainly fierce, which can drive innovation. Banks and credit unions compete fiercely as well. More important to our discussion, these industries frequently foster work environments (and/or have actual processes in place) that welcome or actively solicit ideas from employees on the front line. Seriously considering ideas from front line staff can provide an organization with valuable insight, especially when the competition does not do this.

I regularly experience the tangible effect of both the top-down & bottom-up phenomena when training institutions on the Speak On Purpose strategies outlined in this book. I have trained tellers and bankers with no branch manager in attendance. I have trained entire branches with no regional manager in attendance. I have trained entire regions with no senior manager in attendance. Routinely, we train together, ideas are shared, the staff are excited by the prospect of implementing new strategies and referral activity demonstrably increases. All too often, that is where the excitement ends.

An inclination toward top-down or bottom-up innovation at the institution can become evident during the first requisite follow up meeting with the person who invited me to train. If management upstream was excited to hear about the increased activity, expressed regret at having missed the training and—due to the feedback of staff in attendance—now seek to apply the training to other groups within the institution…bottom-up innovation is probably welcome there. If there is no feedback to report from management upstream, even in light of resulting success in intradepartmental referrals, this may be a top-down institution that is slow to adopt change when the change does not originate at or near the top.

When pressed about a lack of upstream feedback, trainees time and again report seeking to share their success upstream, or cross-stream with peers who were not in attendance, only to be met with resistance. When asked to speculate why they met resistance, sometimes trainees quietly surmise the resistance may be due to ambition (it was not the other person's idea so they do not like it), incredulity (the other person does not believe the training was successful even when shown quantifiable data to the contrary), or resistance to change (the other person expresses distaste for anything unorthodox). As you might imagine, these outcomes frequently serve to demotivate the trainee. He or she abandons the new strategies, even when they were working, and goes back to doing whatever he or she was doing before…which was usually nothing. This is unfortunate and can demotivate the employee in other respects as well.

Fret not however! Top-down organizational structures certainly have their merits. Moreover, Speak On Purpose success is definitely achievable at top-down institutions! When I am asked to speak to boards, senior managers and/or officers and those groups decide to implement the Speak On Purpose program, downstream buy-in of the new strategy is nigh immediate. Accountability can be a challenge during upstream implementation because employees must essentially hold themselves accountable. Effective accountability is typically built-in when an initiative is driven top-down at a financial institution. As a result, Speak On Purpose strategies can be codified and implemented on the front line and throughout the organization. One example of Speak On Purpose accountability and codification entails in-house trainers learning how to train others to speak on purpose, ensuring the strategy is taught to new hires and the expectation to speak on purpose is set early on in an employee's career. Another example involves internally developing and communicating Speak On Purpose criteria to be included in the institution's secret shop process for front line staff evaluation.

The bottom line? If you like what you see as you read this book, or even better, you have already had success implementing anything it, recommend that someone upstream from you go pick up a copy. Your institution, whether top-down or bottom-up, can absolutely work toward building an organizational infrastructure that encourages, nay, insists, on speaking on purpose.

5.2   Why Wear Clothes?

In the previous section, we briefly touched on the merits of upstream or downstream strategic implementation of new ideas. In this section we will cover tactical implementation, particularly as it relates to firmly establishing a process.

Each morning, the vast majority of people wake up and at some point decide what to wear that day. They may put great thought into this decision or they may put very little. Sometimes the decision is made for them to one degree or another (e.g. – a uniform is required). Far less common are people who wake up and decide whether or not they will wear clothes at all. Why?

For humans wearing clothes when you begin your day is a process. Specifically, a process that is drilled into us, essentially from birth. Babies in developed nations are swaddled in clothes and diapers at almost all times, irrespective of the climate. Throughout early childhood, children often instinctively remove their clothes to go play and frolic, giving no care to adult concerns regarding modesty or sexuality. Parents and guardians are reliably there each time to dissuade this behavior in one way or another. Steadily programming the children to follow the process.

Maybe you think humans wear clothes because of society, culture, religion or something along those lines. While those things may be factors to some small degree, the true mechanism by which our behavior in this regard has been effectively altered from birth, is an incessant indoctrination into the process of wearing clothes. Adherence to which, again, must be forced early on. Clothes simply are not natural to living things unless the environment calls for them, in the form of 'natural' clothes such as fur, feathers, bark, etc. With the exception of pets forced to do so by pet owners, other animals do not wear non-naturally occurring clothes as we define them.

Nonetheless, we humans, regardless of society, culture or religion, all eventually capitulate and adopt the clothes-wearing process taught to us. We wear clothes when we start our day and go outside without even considering the alternative.

Now that you are consciously aware of this particular process, here is why it matters. Asking institutions and employees to do things they have never done before (like implementing the Speak On Purpose program) is a tall order. Many financial institutions have existed for decades or centuries and throughout that time tellers and bankers have consistently asked, "Is there anything else I can help you with?" Although various initiatives to refer or cross-sell within the credit union and/or increase the bank's wallet-share have been presented over the years, the status quo remains strong. Inertia (jargon or otherwise) is strong. If you plan to change and your institution plans to change, you and it will need to create then adhere to processes that promote the change that you seek.

This need for processes illustrates another example where top-down buy-in and accountability come into play. Similar to the conscientious guardian always being nearby to help the young one replace his clothes; so too should the front line leaders be there for their peers and employees, reminding them to speak and ask questions on purpose. Similar to how the best parents are encouraging first, only as stern as necessary, and always coming from a place of love; so too should your organization respect that change is difficult, necessary and unlikely to happen overnight.

5.3   Process Best Practices

Best practices for creating and implementing your Speak On Purpose and Ask On Purpose processes may include:

o Developing questions as a collaborative effort,
o Role-playing with co-workers
o Regular follow up and feedback sessions on the efficacy of particular questions
o Mild real-time engagement when a nothing question is overheard (no pestering)
o Empower the front line staff to hold each other accountable
o Make it fun (contests for creative, effective questions and their use)
o Write potential questions to choose from on the break room whiteboard
o Speak on purpose outside of work and as often as possible
o Encourage complete organizational buy-in via training beyond the sales staff

If you and your financial institution consistently coach staff to speak on purpose and ask on purpose while holding all involved accountable, there will no longer be a question of whether or not you ask effective questions. Similar to the daily clothing decision, the only question will be which questions do you ask.

5.4   Manager Best Practices

In section 5.1 I mentioned training employees while the manager was absent. The absence of a manager at a meeting can indicate many things. The most common being that the manager had more pressing matters to attend to but wanted his team to benefit from the training regardless. Though rare, I have found out later that a manager was unaware a training session was being held. Occasionally the manager had determined that the regular training session, which I was simply joining that day, had historically been a waste of his time but was required for his team.

In each instance, the manager is loudly speaking, though probably not purpose, to his or her team. If anything is more important than the staff training and development, the staff want to be at that meeting. If no one thought to tell the manager about the training and the manager did not have a mechanism in place that would assure his awareness

5.5   Real Life Example: Ann

Remember to value each step on the communication hierarchy, even the bottom step. A Teller named Ann attended two early morning Speak On Purpose trainings in her branch where Module 1 was covered. She did not change her behavior. When asked why during a follow up discussion with the Lead Teller, Ann said, "I'm too nervous to ask customers about anything else. They're just here to make a deposit." Ann's anxiety about moving up the hierarchy had her stuck on the ground floor of No Communication. The teller supervisor, Ann and I worked together to help her take the first step, Written Communication. She began providing the personal banker's business card and the bank's lending services rack brochure insert with each transaction receipt. Sometimes clients asked her about the literature and she became more comfortable with answering that simple inquiry. Importantly, working together we were able to improve Ann's sales communication standard from nothing to something.

Ann's anxiety resulted in her refusal to accept that, by communicating something beyond the transaction, she was potentially helping a customer by leading them toward a solution. The oft repeated Henry Ford adage comes to mind: "People don't know what they want until you show them" (Henry Ford, 1910; see also variations commonly attributed to Steve Jobs, 2011). Speak On Purpose taught Ann how to use the first step up the communication hierarchy, written communication in the form of business cards and brochures, as a crutch to help her help others. As she gained confidence, she was later able to step up once again and communicate verbally in a sales environment— something she swore she would never do.

5.6   Real Life Example: Jen

Increasing referrals in the financial industry is not always about financial acumen or workplace policy. Jen was an experienced banker who had no qualms with following the rules. Her referral activity had never been noteworthy however and her manager believed that doing better in that regard would help Jen toward her goal of being promoted. After discreetly observing Jen working with customers and taking notes about those interactions, we had our initial one-on-one training session. As I sat in the branch manager's office and watched Jen with 4 different customers, it appeared she was making several unforced, non-verbal errors that could be addressed by the concepts introduced in Module 1 of this book.

Initially, Jen was dismissive when asked about her referral activity. She explained that she always made mention of value-added services provided by the bank, customers simply never responded. In fact, she showed me her well-worn script for bringing up additional services that she had developed years prior, after a different training initiative at the bank. While the script seldom resulted in a referral, Jen held herself accountable to implementing bank initiatives, which is commendable.

Implement On Purpose

After covering Speak On Purpose Module 1 with her, I tactfully walked Jen through my observations regarding her non-verbal communication and proposed a game plan that, if implemented would likely bring the referral success she sought. I described how her non-verbal cues were clearly visible from where I had sat in the branch manager's office and therefore those same cues were undoubtedly being read by the customer in her office. I explained how these non-verbal signals were impacting her referral success, though she continued to express skepticism. How could controlling such things as frequency and duration of eye contact, when and whether to lean forward, and how often and to what degree she raised or lowered her eyebrows have any impact on whether a client met with a financial advisor?

Nevertheless, with the manager's support, Jen committed to developing and implementing her unique plan to be purposeful in her non-verbal communication. The plan was designed specifically to elicit the following from customers: stronger connections, more trust and greater belief that Jen had their best interests at heart. Upon implementation, Jen saw considerably more success in customers expressing interest in, and taking follow up meetings to discuss, additional services offered by the bank. In her own words, Jen was astonished at how such small changes had such a profound impact.

5.7   Embracing Objections

In section 2.11 I introduced the concept of embracing objections versus overcoming them. I briefly outlined the embracing process, as taught to me by poet and consultant, Julian Curry: 1) Repeat objections back to the customer to confirm you heard it the way they meant it. 2) Acknowledge that you understand and appreciate their concerns. 3) Detail to the client how you plan to address their concerns. Here we will dive deeper into this process as it will be imperative.

Figure 5
(Source: https://digitalsynopsis.com/buzz/not-my-job-funny-pics/)

5.8   Reflections on Module 5

The image above (*see figure 5*) has stuck with me since the first time I saw it. It was the first image that appeared in 2007 when I Googled,

"Not My Job" as I prepared for a presentation on employee motivation. Sometimes an employee thinks some aspect of his job (e.g. – asking questions) is not actually part of the job, because the aspect is not clearly defined in the job description. I routinely meet bank employees who have never actually asked a potentially helpful question or made a referral. In nearly every instance, that employee has also never been held accountable for this inaction. Asking potentially helpful questions is clearly part of working at any financial institution in a customer-facing role. If you are a leader, identify team members who mistakenly think asking potentially helpful questions is not their job. Once identified, begin introducing them to the Speak On Purpose program. Better yet, have them pick up a copy of this book!

- Nearly every working adult has heard the expression, "Don't judge a book by its cover." Moreover, most businesspeople claim to understand the expression and adhere to it. Nevertheless, it remains widespread financial institution practice (though not policy) to essentially disqualify customers based on superficial observations alone. In these instances, customers are not even asked a question regarding some additional service because some aspect(s) of their appearance is deemed unsuitable. This common implementation failure can be mitigated. Virtually any bank or credit union veteran has a true story of a customer who dressed, acted or even smelled like a vagrant but was in fact very well off. Similarly, many communities have at least one true story about someone everyone in the community believed penniless, yet upon their passing the deceased was found to have possessed significant wealth. When implementing the Ask On Purpose curriculum, task veterans or managers with periodically sharing these stories with their teams to ensure all opportunities are uncovered. Let the customer disqualify themselves, do not do it for them. Besides, if you treat the customer with respect and assume they may qualify for all of your services, when they receive a windfall they will remember which institution treated them with respect...and which ones did not.

- Branch break rooms often contain magazines brought from home and announcements related to the institution or community. Consider placing one or two single-page, graphic-heavy financial literacy pieces in the same area as the magazines and/or announcements. (Nothing specific to your institution). There is no need to publicize or explain the presence of these items. If one employee notices one item and learns one new thing...mission accomplished. Often, effective questions are formed when a new idea is introduced via self-discovery.

- When you perceive implementing change at your institution to be particularly difficult for whatever reason, consider the 'power of three.' Many sources can be found that will expound on this psychological and somewhat mystical concept. Personally, I have found it quite effective and do not need to know the specifics as to why. As it relates to the curriculum in this book, pick one module and break it into three stages (introduction, execution, follow-up). You can implement the same module repeatedly for regular new hires and/or move to a new module once the previous module has been mastered at your institution. Regardless, implement on purpose.

Thank you for joining me on this journey! Whether you are at work or at home, whether you are engaging with someone in-person or over the phone, whether you are leaving a voicemail or setting your outgoing greeting…remember to **Speak On Purpose**.

If you enjoyed this book,

keep an eye out for the next volume in the series,

"Control What You Can Control"

by Marlōn Hall, AS, BS, CFS

APPENDIX A: Speak to Yourself On Purpose

"Give me a stock clerk with a goal and I will give you a man who will make history. Give me a man without a goal and I will give you a stock clerk."

–J. C. Penney

I fully credit world renowned authors and motivational speakers Brian Tracy and Dr. Kevin Elko with my personal process for goal realization. Brian Tracy's audiobook, "Goals! How to Get Everything You Want – Faster than You Ever Thought Possible" was, and remains, instrumental in every aspect of my professional career success. Furthermore, Mr. Tracy's daily goal review constitutes the foundation of my personal goal process outlined here.

Hearing Dr. Kevin Elko speak for the first time in 2010 convinced me that it was time to stop considering and start doing. Hearing him repeatedly over the years taught me that how I spoke to myself was even more important than how I spoke to others. In this section, I simply explain to you my process, which I developed by following the guidance of these great leaders. This is how and why I speak to myself on purpose.

A.1 Morning & Evening Goals

Each morning, immediately upon waking, I reach for a writing utensil of any kind and something on which to write. I endeavor to have a notepad and pen at hand specific to this purpose, however sometimes I do not, for a variety of reasons. Regardless, before my toiletries or calisthenics or even kissing my wife, I write down my daily goals. As I write them down, I vocalize them. Once complete, I read the goals from start to finish and vocalize them again.

Each evening, before I finally close my eyes, I repeat the process. I endeavor to do this just before I go to sleep, which can be quite tricky. If at any point before actually sleeping, I judge the risk of dozing off before I complete my goals to be too great, I complete my goal process then and there. I stop my late-night working, emailing, reading, eating, etc. and pick up the writing utensil and writing surface and complete my goal process.

A.2 Learning Modalities

My process of writing the goals, voicing the goals and reading the goals, stems from research related to learning modalities or learning styles. Three of the most common styles are tactile, visual and auditory. Writing the goals of course being tactile, reading them being visual and speaking them aloud being auditory. Learning styles are used to describe which of the five senses a learner uses primarily when he or she is learning new information. Seeing, hearing and touching being more common learning styles because learning via smelling and tasting largely limits one to learning only smells and tastes.

Education research indicates each human has a primary or preferred style. Educators can instruct on purpose in a variety of styles in an effort to reach as many students as possible. Writing, reading and voicing my goals aloud ensures they are being received by my subconscious via each distinct mode. A great deal of research has been done on learning modalities and there is some belief that different genders prefer one style over another. Regardless, covering the big three makes the most sense to me. Indeed, several of my professors at the University of Wyoming specifically outlined their intent at the beginning of their course to teach in as many styles as possible to ensure each student absorbed the material being taught as effectively as possible. Since my goals are at least as important to me as anything I learned in college, I speak to myself the same way.

A.3   Goal Programming

When I complete my goals in the morning, I am purposefully placing them into my subconscious before the endless demands on my attention and distractions of the day begin. Before I check emails, before I check messages, before I check anything. I am specifically placing these most important (to me) ideas into my 'fresh from dreaming' mind. To use a computer analogy, I am programming my subconscious to start the day.

When I complete my goals at night, I am again purposefully placing them into my subconscious, this time before I go to sleep. The subconscious mind is purported to take complete control when one sleeps and I want to direct mine toward my goals as best I can. I am programming my subconscious as I begin the nightly dream cycle. Other things I do at night to increase the efficacy of my programming include mild sensory deprivation (e.g. – no to light or screens, yes to white noise) and 65° Fahrenheit room temperature (when room temperature is within my control). Much medical and scientific research has gone into ideal sleep conditions for REM sleep and I adhere to those research findings as often as I can.

Using three learning modalities is also a form of programming. If I analogize each modality with a programming language, then I am programming goals into my subconscious mind with triple redundancy. Each message should therefore be reinforced and more likely to be processed.

A.4   Goal Formatting

When formatting my goals, I follow Brian Tracy's 3P's rule. Goals must be personal, positive and present tense. The personal format means my goals often start with "I" and are about me and mine (e.g. – "I am strong and healthy."). The positive format means my goals are about what I want and never about what I do not want (I would not say, "I am not sick and weak.") Lastly, the present tense format means my goals seek to bring the future into the now (I would not write, "I will be strong and healthy.")

Over the years I have added 2 more P rules for my own use, passionate and precise. Each goal of mine must be something that I sincerely care about. I do not want to waste this powerful tool on frivolous or ephemeral desires. Also I believe that programming my goals with passion makes the programming more effective. Finally, each goal must be specific, I prefer targeted goals versus vague or broad goals. Personal, positive, present, passionate and precise...this is how I speak to myself on purpose every morning and every night.

A.5   Examples

In this section you will see small sampling of my goals, lifted from many notebooks kept over many years. Yours must be your own. These are simply listed to illustrate my personal process.

- o I am strong and healthy.
- o I make wise and excellent decisions.
- o I am focused and disciplined.
- o I am an ideal husband and father.
- o I am well-rested and well-prepared.
- o My family is safe and happy.
- o I am a compelling and dynamic public speaker.
- o I live long and prosper.

o I am independently wealthy.

o My willpower is limitless.

o I accomplish all of my goals.

I generally place the last goal, "I accomplish all of my goals," at the end of my other goals where it serves as a final instruction to my subconscious to 'get it all done.' The number of goals vary from time to time and the nature of my goals often change depending on my circumstances, though some goals have remained constant since I began this process. I speak to myself on purpose. I suggest you do the same.

A.6   Reflections on Appendix A

- When voicing my goals, sometimes I whisper so as not to wake my wife. Other times when I am alone I shout, when I am particularly passionate and I want to express myself thus.

- I have trained my sons on this goal process from a very young age and they now take this process for granted and have made it their own, something for which I am eternally grateful.

- Though rare, sometimes I do not have tools to write my goals. When that is the case, I still voice my goals aloud. One style is better than none.

- In those exceedingly rare instances when I can neither write nor speak when programming myself with my goals, I articulate them in my mind as a litany. Prayers, litanies and mantras, while normally directed outside ourselves to higher powers or the universe at large, still represent a form of speaking to ourselves. Are we not one with the universe or at least a part of it? Is God not inside each of us? If not, should we not let him in? Either way, English political theorist Algernon Sidney said, "God helps those who help themselves."

- Buy Brian Tracy's audiobook or book today for his entire Goal Development process, I have not even scratched the surface here.

- In addition to daily goals, a few years back I added the citing of daily gratitude to my process after hearing from numerous speakers and authors how valuable this tool was. I can now attest to the value of this exercise. Articulating the things for which I am grateful each day lessens any natural penchant for complaining and has improved my mood in general. For example, when people cut me off in traffic, I am less likely to express frustration because I can easily call to mind how grateful I am there was no accident or injury.

- Even when a particular goal has been achieved, I often continue to record it in order to maintain its achievement.

- A daily goal, in the context of this appendix, is defined as a goal written down daily. Daily written goals in fact include short term, mid-term, long term and ongoing life goals. Whether it is daily, weekly, quarterly, yearly, five years, ten years, fifty years, etc., if you want your goal programmed into your subconscious, speak to yourself on purpose.

APPENDIX B: Why Do You Say That?

Idioms are common in everyday speech and because this book is titled Speak On Purpose, in this section we take a brief look at the original purpose of a few common phrases.

Knock on wood: This phrase/action is said to have originated in ancient Celtic cultures which spread out across Europe during the Bronze and Iron Ages (3500 BCE – 700 CE). These cultures are said to have held a close affinity with woodlands, which were far more abundant at that time. The phrase/action 'knock on wood' is said to ward off bad luck or thank the spirits for good luck. The Ash, the Oak and the Hawthorn tree are particularly sacred in ancient Irish lore.

Don't burn your bridges: This phrase is said to have originated in ancient Rome (753 BCE – 476 CE). During Roman military campaigns, commanders were reported to have ordered that bridges be burned to eliminate the possibility of retreat forcing the soldiers to either win or die. Bridges were also reportedly burned to prevent the escape of enemies. In modern usage, the phrase often refers to doing irreversibly ruining a relationship.

Why Do You Say That?

<u>Your ears must be burning</u>: This phrase also originates in the ancient Roman Empire where it was believed that feelings in certain parts of the body were messages about current or future events. Specifically, a burning sensation in your ear indicated that you were being discussed. Furthermore, it was believed that burning in your right ear meant you were being praised, while burning in your left ear meant you were being criticized.

<u>Once in a blue moon</u>: This phrase has its modern origins in the Maine Farmers' Almanac. Since 1819, the almanac has designated the third full moon in a four full moon season the 'blue moon.' Such full moons are rare and only occur when there are thirteen full moons in a year instead of the more common twelve. In medieval England circa the late 1500s, 'blue moon' referred to something impossible, not only something very rare. It took centuries for the meaning 'blue moon' to shift from impossible to very rare.

<u>Keep an eye out</u>: This phrase finds its origins with sailors using their spyglasses in the early 1600s. Spyglasses had 3X and 4X magnification and were most often used to spy land while sailing, long before land could be seen by the naked eye. They were also used in military applications to see enemy vessels too far away for the naked eye. In modern usage the phrase refers to being watchful for someone or something, often while doing some other primary task.

Why Do You Say That?

While spyglasses are also called telescopes, Galileo did not invent them. He simply modified and improved them and pointed them skyward instead of landward. Spyglasses themselves had been modified from an already centuries old invention, reading glasses. Since using the spyglass required only one eye, the phrase 'keep an eye out' was born.

Even when using idioms or common phrases, speak on purpose!

This page intentionally left blank.

ACKNOWLEDGEMENTS

I am immeasurably grateful to my wife, primary editor and research librarian Snow Marlonsson, MLIS for her unconditional love, forbearance and insight, all of which made this a better book. My gratitude further extends to editor Scott Forbes and each of the following individuals for playing an integral role in the development of this content over the course of many years: Rosemary Hall, Lucille Byrd, Brook Young, Ares Marlōnsson, Rameses Marlōnsson, Damon Hall, Sr., The Rutschman-Bylers, The Piechockis, Jiryu Mark, Frank Lambrecht, Adolph Peavy, Sifu Jerry, Sensei Robin Swank, Sharon Hand, Christine Stebbins, Celise Swanson, Richard Rodriguez, Julie Bromley, Gary Negich, Dan Emborg, Gary Crum, Ronna Voges, Kim Funchess, Chris Wesner, Barry Lowery, Wesley Vance, Mark Zinder, Julian Curry, Andre Dowtin, Michael Helgeson, Nicole Gouthro-Perry, Anthony Cillo, Rick Parker, Florence Huang, Bri Means, Greg Cicotte, Scott Romine, Marc Socol, Dan Starishevsky, Phil Wright, Paul Napolitano, Elizabeth Griffith, Suzy Thompson, Traci Anderson, Tamu McCreary, Chardae Hawley, Dawn Foster, Joy Orlando, TJ Williams, Matt Gill and many, many, many others who have inspired me, encouraged me, helped me, taught me, mentored me, nurtured me, hired me, promoted me, saved me, held me accountable, befriended me and loved me.

ABOUT THE AUTHOR

Marlōn Hall is a business consultant, corporate trainer and professional speaker working primarily with financial services organizations. While his Speak On Purpose training curriculum has been outlined in this primer with financial institutions in mind, the program and its myriad concepts may be applied to nearly any client-facing industry.

Mr. Hall graduated from Laramie County Community College and the University of Wyoming and received his professional designation from the Institute of Business and Finance. He has been a sales professional for over 20 years who today works primarily with financial institutions and independent insurance agencies. He is also the founder of the Association for Wholesaling Diversity.

Mr. Hall was born and raised by a single mother, in the Roseland neighborhood on the south side of Chicago. He is a father of three, grandfather of two and husband of one.

To ask questions and/or schedule consultant, training or speaking services please direct all correspondence to:

Phone: 303.242.0948

Email: speakonpurpose@gmail.com

THANK YOU!!!

MAKE IT A PROSPEROUS DAY!!!

SOURCES & ANNOTATIONS

Ajayi, L. (2016). Get comfortable with being uncomfortable.
https://www.ted.com/talks/luvvie_ajayi_get_comfortable_with_being_unc
omfortable?language=en&utm_campaign=tedspread&utm_medium=referr
al&utm_source=tedcomshare

Cameron K.S., Quinn R.E. (2011). Business and Economics. John Wiley & Sons.

Cavicchio, Federica, et al. "Compositionality in the Language of Emotion." *PLoS
ONE*, vol. 13, no. 8, Aug. 2018, pp. 1–19. *EBSCOhost*,
doi:10.1371/journal.pone.0201970.

Cullen, M. (2018). 127 Top Business jargon examples: And how to fix them.
Instructional solutions. From
https://www.instructionalsolutions.com/blog/jargon

Duhig, C. (1014). The Power of habit: Why we do what we do in life and business.
Random House LLC. New York, New York.

Fawcett, H., Oldfield, J. (2016). Investigating expectations and experiences of audio
and written assignment feedback in first-year undergraduate
students. *Teaching In Higher Education*, *21*(1), 79-93.
doi:10.1080/13562517.2015.1115969

Ford, W. S. Z. (2001). Customer Expectations for Interactions with Service Providers:
Relationship Versus Encounter.. *Journal of Applied Communication
Research*, *29*(1), 1. Retrieved from
http://search.ebscohost.com/login.aspx?direct=true&AuthType=cookie,ip,c
pid&custid=s9038647&db=aph&AN=4157779&site=ehost-live

Ford, W. S. Z., & Etienne, C. N. (1994). Can I Help You?: A Framework for the
Interdisciplinary Research on Customer Service Encounters. Management
Communication Quarterly, 7(4), 413–441.
https://doi.org/10.1177/0893318994007004003

Frost, R. A., & Monaghan, P. (2017). Sleep-Driven Computations in Speech
Processing. *Plos ONE*, *12*(1), 1-14. doi:10.1371/journal.pone.0169538

Fulghum, R. (2004). All I really need to know I learned in kindergarten: Uncommon thoughts on common things. Random House Publishing Group. New York, NY. ISBN 0345479106, 9780345479105

Hall, M. (2019). How to Ensure You're Ignored By Clients: Jargon gets in the way of effective communication. From: https://401kspecialistmag.com/how-to-ensure-youre-ignored-by-clients/

Hellman, P. (2017). You've Got 8 Seconds: Communication Secrets for a Distracted World. (2017). TD: Talent Development, 71(5), 67. Retrieved from https://tinyurl.com/y69bj8fd

Holmes, O.W. GoodReads Find Quotes accessed 2018 from https://tinyurl.com/yyr3hkyc

Keith, Nina, et al. "Informal Learning and Entrepreneurial Success: A Longitudinal Study of Deliberate Practice among Small Business Owners." *Applied Psychology: An International Review*, vol. 65, no. 3, July 2016, pp. 515–540. *EBSCOhost*, doi:10.1111/apps.12054.

Kevoe-Feldman, H. (2015). What Can You Do for Me? Communication Methods Customers Use to Solicit Personalization within the Service Encounter. *Communication Monographs*, *82*(4), 510–534. https://doi.org/10.1080/03637751.2015.1024916

Knauf, H. (2016). Reading, listening and feeling: audio feedback as a component of an inclusive learning culture at universities. *Assessment & Evaluation In Higher Education*, *41*(3), 442-449. doi:10.1080/02602938.2015.1021664

Koppensteiner, Markus, and Greg Siegle. "Speaking through the Body." *Politics & the Life Sciences*, vol. 36, no. 2, Fall 2017, pp. 104–113. *EBSCOhost*, doi:10.1017/pls.2017.23.

Lane, Joel A. "The Imposter Phenomenon Among Emerging Adults Transitioning Into Professional Life: Developing a Grounded Theory." *Adultspan Journal*, vol. 14, no. 2, Oct. 2015, pp. 114–128. *EBSCOhost*, doi:10.1002/adsp.12009.

Maney, K. (2015). The Eight-Second Genius. *Newsweek Global*, *164*(17), 48–49. Retrieved from http://search.ebscohost.com/login.aspx?direct=true&AuthType=cookie,ip,cpid&custid=s9038647&db=aph&AN=102207161&site=ehost-live

Martinez, L., Falvello, V. B., Aviezer, H., & Todorov, A. (2016). Contributions of facial expressions and body language to the rapid perception of dynamic emotions. *Cognition & Emotion*, *30*(5), 939-952. doi:10.1080/02699931.2015.1035229

McDonough, J., Egolf, K. (2015). The advertising age encyclopedia of advertising. Routledge. New York, New York.

Medler-Liraz, H., & Yagil, D. (2013). Customer Emotion Regulation in the Service Interactions: Its Relationship to Employee Ingratiation, Satisfaction and Loyalty Intentions. *Journal of Social Psychology*, *153*(3), 261–278. https://doi.org/10.1080/00224545.2012.729105

Meis, J., & Kashima, Y. (2017). Signage as a tool for behavioral change: Direct and indirect routes to understanding the meaning of a sign. *Plos ONE*, *12*(8), 1-16. doi:10.1371/journal.pone.0182975

Morioka, Shu, et al. "Incongruence between Verbal and Non-Verbal Information Enhances the Late Positive Potential." *PLoS ONE*, vol. 11, no. 10, Oct. 2016, pp. 1–11. *EBSCOhost*, doi:10.1371/journal.pone.0164633.

Pilcher, J. (2014. Say it again: Messages are more effective when repeated. The Financial Brand. From https://thefinancialbrand.com/42323/advertising-marketing-messages-effective-frequency/

Seta, J. J., & Seta, C. E. (1992). Personal Equity-Comparison Theory: An Analysis of Value and the Generation of Compensatory and Noncompensatory Expectancies. *Basic & Applied Social Psychology*, *13*(1), 47–66. Retrieved from http://search.ebscohost.com/login.aspx?direct=true&AuthType=cookie,ip,c pid&custid=s9038647&db=aph&AN=7301522&site=ehost-live

Sluzki, Carlos E. "Proxemics in Couple Interactions: Rekindling an Old Optic." *Family Process*, vol. 55, no. 1, Mar. 2016, pp. 7–15. *EBSCOhost*, doi:10.1111/famp.12196.

Smith, J. (2013). 10 Nonverbal cues that convey confidence at work. Forbes. From https://www.forbes.com/sites/jacquelynsmith/2013/03/11/10-nonverbal-cues-that-convey-confidence-at-work/#4bebfad25e13

Smith, T., Osborne, J.H. (1886). Successful advertising: Its secrets explained. Bazaar Press, London England.

Strauss, S. (2018). In era of short attention spans, try to stand out. USA Today. Retrieved from http://search.ebscohost.com/login.aspx?direct=true&AuthType=cookie,ip,c pid&custid=s9038647&db=aph&AN=J0E047518680518&site=ehost-live

Teixeira, T. (2015). When people pay attention to video ads and why. From https://tinyurl.com/ouymmnv

Cover Image: Design/Layout by Snow Marlonsson | Photo by Traci Anderson, Murrieta, CA | Custom Suit by Threaded NYC

Appendix B: Wood: https://ireland-calling.com/celtic-mythology-trees/

Appendix B: Bridges: https://grammarist.com/idiom/burn-ones-bridges-and-burn-ones-boats/

Appendix B: Ears: https://www.bloomsbury-international.com/en/student-ezone/idiom-of-the-week/list-of-itioms/1235-my-ears-are-burning/

Appendix B: Moon: https://www.phrases.org.uk/meanings/once-in-a-blue-moon.html

Appendix B: Spyglass: https://www.bloomsbury-international.com/en/student-ezone/idiom-of-the-week/list-of-idioms/1205-keep-an-eye-out/

Appendix B: Spyglass: https://theamericanscholar.org/galileos-spyglass/#.XLzjeFRKjDc

Clipart: Figure 3 pointing finger: https://commons.wikimedia.org/wiki/File:Finger-pointing-icon.png

Clipart: Figure 3 thumbs up: https://commons.wikimedia.org/wiki/File:Thumbs-up-icon-left.svg

Clipart: Figure 3 open palm: https://www.flickr.com/photos/plaisanter/5289014766/

Clipart: Figure 1 ear: shutterstock 219495679: https://publicdomainpictures.net/en/view-image.php?image=15450&picture=lyssnande-ora

Clipart: Ares: https://en.wikipedia.org/wiki/File:Mars_symbol.svg

Clipart: Ra: http://www.thestillman.com/stillmanfiles/page/3/

Clipart: Snowflake: https://openclipart.org/detail/189610/snowflake-9

To maintain SPEAK ON PURPOSE'S role as a quick primer for sales communication, we have sequestered much of the academic backstory here, in the notes:

According to Martinez, et. al, (2016), participants detected the emotions: anger, disgust, fear and surprise by viewing an actor's body alone, better in 250 milliseconds than in 500 milliseconds, 2 seconds and 4 seconds. They detected happiness equally well in 250 milliseconds and detected sadness better in the longer, <250 milliseconds test. The 250 millisecond test results applied equally to body-only and head-only images.

Meish and Kashima's 2017 study on the effectiveness of signage on behavior change finds that signage is a prompt to act on a behavior that already exists in your clients' mind. Equally important; signage should be near the place of action and give specific directions, in either polite or demanding tone (research shows that tone is irrelevant to behavior change). For example, instead of displaying a sign about a new or unfamiliar behavior: "Meet with our financial adviser NOW", display this instead "Get yourself a pension by meeting Doug NOW". Pensions are familiar. Doug is a specific person. Doing *something for yourself* is a familiar behavior that already exists.

Ford and Jobs use of this common phrase.

Rob Dearman is Managing Partner and Chief Information Officer for F3 Logic.

Koppensteiner and Siegle's, 2017 research on body language concluded that listening comprehension is multi-modal. Providing the sound of writing to a person over the phone is like adding a physical gesture, the effect of which is adding a layer of cognitive confirmation. The research team found that gestures precede speech by microseconds, signaling what the listener should expect (and helping the speaker access his vocabulary). When gestures and words convey identical meanings; comprehension rises markedly. Experiments to test listener comprehension with and without gestures and context emerged in 1951 with Ruesch & Bateson's 1951 study and gained momentum into the 1970's. Today, research such as Koppensteiner and Siegle's measures the effect of minute gestural changes on cognition by separating audio from speech, codifying gestures and comparing participant perceptions.

Carlos Sluzki's 2016 article about proxemics summarizes the evolution of the study of interpersonal proximity between individuals. To summarize, your clients are attaching meaning to the distance you maintain from their body, based largely on an internalized, culturally inspired filter. I recommend that you familiarize yourself with his research before your next meeting.

Supplementary keywords: psychological ownership, territoriality, metaperception

"Control what you can control." While the call center reps cannot control the customers' initial negative emotional eruption, they can control how they interpret the outburst, their role in the interaction and even their feelings and expectations. I use this mantra in every aspect of my life and it will most likely be the topic of my next publication. I succeeded in a negative environment by using customer dissatisfaction as an opportunity to be their hero. If I could solve their problem by controlling what I could control (and letting go of everything else) our interaction was even more impactful than if they started from a *mildly dissatisfied* position.

To learn more about bringing the learner mindset to work, enjoy this pithy video:
https://www.ted.com/talks/eduardo_briceno_how_to_get_better_at_the_things_yo u_care_about?utm_campaign=tedspread&utm_medium=referral&utm_source=tedc omshare

See also Gardner's 1961 Social Exchange Theory and keywords: emotional labor, opinions conformity and organizational display rules.

The field of Social Psychology begins to explore ideas surrounding interpersonal imbalance in the 1950's beginning with research by Festinger (1957) and Aronson and Mills (1959). Their hypothesis; cost incurrence increases perceived value, was seminal because it predated cognitive theory. To summarize, "Personal equity-comparison theory addresses how [...] events influence expectations about future events. These expectations, in turn, are assumed to influence the perceived value of obtained outcomes through simple comparison processes (Seta & Seta 1992)". And the comparison relevant to SPEAK ON PURPOSE is the social dynamic of the service relationship as expressed through conversation. See also: compensatory expectation and ceiling value.

This page intentionally left blank.

EPILOGUE

"Speaking on purpose is only the beginning. Do all things deliberately. Think on purpose, act on purpose, live on purpose!"

—*Ramesēs A. Marlōnsson*

TheNatureOfAThought

A poem by Ramesēs A. Marlōnsson

uponcompletioniwouldfeelaserenitylikenoother

alascompletionwillneveroccur

thoughtscannotfinish

theyclogthemindthepaperthetongue

thoughts linger on

unrelentingintheir continuity

but imagine,

what the mind, paper and tongue might look like

upon completion of a thought…

f r e e

NOTES

NOTES

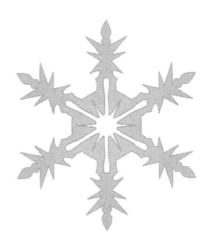

All Things Are Possible.

We Know Nothing.

Made in the USA
Lexington, KY
26 November 2019